The BETOOTA ADVOCATE

HOW GOOD'S AUSTRALIA

Pan Macmillan Australia

THE BETOOTA ADVOCATE is a small and independent regional newspaper from far west Queensland. We pride ourselves on reporting fair and just news with an authenticity that rivals only the salt on the sunburnt earth that surrounds us here in the Queensland Channel Country.

Having been established in the mid-1800s, we are arguably Australia's oldest newspaper and have always taken pride in our ability to walk in both worlds: regional and metropolitan news. In recent times, our popularity has grown immensely as a result of a bold move to create an online revival for our publication.

CLANCY OVERELL

Born on V-J Day in 1945 to a staunchly Methodist temperance-league-organiser mother and a lapsed Catholic newspaper-baron father, Clancy Overell was a result of his family's last crack at a male heir – in an effort to protect four generations of blatant patriarchal media nepotism that had proven fruitful for them since the first barrel of ink.

Luckily for the Overells, their son showed no interest in law, medicine or Duntroon and was ready for a reporting cadetship shortly after confirmation.

Despite the promise of a job for life, Clancy took several brief sabbaticals from the media publishing game in his early adulthood. First, he explored the possibility of playing professional rugby league, before a disgusting compound fracture to both his tib and fib during the Betoota Dolphins 1965 grand final loss to the Cunnamulla Rams steered him back to the less physically-exerting brand of alcoholism known as journalism. He took off again to join Jimmy Sharman's Boxing Tent, building a résumé through the grog and head knocks that eventually landed him a job as lead media advisor for the Sir Joh government. This career tangent wrapped up after Overell's then-fiancée's house was raided as part of the sensationalist left wing witch-hunt known as the Fitzgerald Inquiry.

He then returned to Channel Country to take up the editor role left empty by his retiring father. He has remained in that role ever since.

ERROL PARKER

Born in Hong Kong on 2 April 1977 into a middle-class family in Wan Chai, the only child of Gigi Lau, a Cathay Pacific stewardess and Schalk Parker, a Namibian arms dealer and Namibian War of Independence veteran.

Following high school at Sheng Kung Hui Tang Shiu Kin Secondary School, Parker found work as a copy boy at the *South China Morning Post* in 1995. At age 20, Parker met esteemed Australian journalist Murray Sayle at the 1997 Handover Ceremony, who urged him to take a position at *The Sun* in the United Kingdom.

After close to ten years at *The Sun*, Parker was recruited to its sister paper, *News of the World*. It was at this paper that the high-water mark of Parker's career was recorded until he was indicted with a string of criminal offences during the 2011–12 Leveson Inquiry, which ultimately brought an end to his time in the United Kingdom.

In 2014, after working as a keeper at West Falkland lighthouse and sailing around the South Pacific, Parker arrived in Australia, which lead him to answer an ad in *The Courier-Mail*. The ad was written by Dr Clancy Overell OAM, who was looking for a senior journalist with 'tabloid experience'.

NOTE: In light of recent defamation victories in the federal courts, legal counsel for our humble regional newspaper has redacted several passages and articles in this book. We at The Betoota Advocate *see this as blatant censorship – and the dawn of a new age – where silencing the media has become the norm for the class traitors the make up the Australian legal system. This is the reality that you, the reader, must come to accept.*

CONTENTS

INTRODUCTION

THE INVENTION OF THE 24-HOUR NEWS CYCLE has left us with more gaffes than footpaths. It's maligned our sports stars. It's broken many of our elected officials. It's changed the way we view and respond to science, art, information and entertainment.

The only thing that can cut through is a slogan.

Like a policeman remembering to turn the bodycam off when the baton comes out, slogans to a politician are second nature. They're almost always the product of a creative mind, or a whole room of them. Doctors of spin. Admen who know more about ourselves than we do. They take time and patience, focus groups and rounds of graphic design. The process of creating a political slogan begins well before the election date is scribbled atop the nation's chalkboard.

But in the shady world of political slogans and spin, the evening of 18 May 2019 stands out for all Australians.

It was supposed to be Bill Shorten's ascension into our nation's long and storied history, to be cast in stone as a leader of men, until humanity's last hour. To prove once and for all that he wasn't going to be remembered as Victoria's answer to Kim Beazley. He had already risen above the political milk that was Crean and Rudd – Bill Shorten was cream, to be poured lovingly into the chalice of democracy.

By comparison, Scott Morrison was a room-temperature mug of caffeinated banana-flavoured milk.

It was Scott, better known locally by his stage name 'ScoMo', who somehow found his bum on the last seat left in a largely pathetic game of musical chairs. His predecessor, Malcolm Turnbull, was already walking out of the party. Tony Abbott had been ejected by the host's parents for shitting on the rug, and Peter Dutton, who at one point had a bum cheek on the last seat, had fallen back onto the floor where he started the game. All the while Bill was in the next room chatting to parents and trying to impress them by reciting the tricky seven times table.

Little did young Billy know, he was getting nearly every multiplication wrong. Only a few parents dared to correct him and when they did, they were immediately condemned by the others for being unsupportive.

Which brings us back to the events of 18 May.

On election day, ScoMo is out and about near his home in Sydney's Southern Districts, waving and smiling. To the casual onlooker, it looks like Scott is enjoying his twilight in the nation's cockpit. Looking back on his career and looking forward to

what the future holds. Will he go back to running tourism campaigns? Unlikely. Perhaps he'll try his hand at being a consultant slash advisor at a large bank? Maybe. Or will he stay on in politics until what happened to Malcolm happens to him? A certainty.

ScoMo watches the sun dip behind the Great Dividing Range on the night of 18 May and knows that when it reappears up over the Tasman Sea in the morning, he'll still be Prime Minister. Early internal party polling suggests that Queenslanders aren't going to flip on the Coalition. This election will be more than trying to win Western Sydney or the bushy fringes of Melbourne. But that's a whole other story.

When the sun sets, the prime ministerial BMW pulls up at the Morrisons' and a plain-clothed member of ScoMo's protection detail yells up the stairs that the car is here.

He hasn't been allowed to move into Kirribilli House yet. Only the night's winner will get the honour. Scott is brushing his teeth. He looks at himself in the mirror of his upstairs bathroom, grabs his powder-blue tie with one hand and spits the Macleans into the basin. With the back of his tie, he wipes the excess toothpaste off his face and begins the long walk down the stairs and into the purring 7 Series at the end of his garden path.

Scott watches the streetlights whip by overhead as he moves at speed northwards to the Liberal Party function in Sydney's big smoke district. The Prime Minister's team trails behind in an eggshell-white BMW four-wheel-drive, putting together a victory speech and a concession speech at the same time. As history now tells, they are wasting their time.

As the night rolls on, it quickly becomes clear that Scott Morrison is about to be elected as leader of our billycart of a national democracy, about to hurtle down a steep hill with only a pair of well-worn Clarke's school shoes to use as brakes.

The phone rings in his chief of staff's pocket. 'It's Bill Shorten, Mr Prime Minister,' he might say. Scott takes the phone and speaks into it for 40 seconds without really saying anything worth remembering.

The victory is his. Someone in a suit on stage calls his name.

As he starts the long walk up to the stage, he's handed the victory speech his team of creative doctors of spin have handcrafted for the occasion. Two sheets of A4 paper in an outstretched hand just off the side of the stage. Written down are slogans and key points. Things to cover and people to thank.

Scott pushes the pages aside and continues onto the stage, waving and smiling so hard he's almost laughing at how absurd the whole spectacle is.

Now at the lectern, he lets out a cheerful sigh of relief, licks his lips and presents the nation with a rhetorical question. One that has now transcended into eternal slogandom. One that could've immediately followed the 'Where the bloody hell are ya?' Lara Bingle asked the world under his tenure as Head of Tourism Australia.

'How Good's Australia?'

'How Good are Australians?'

The Betoota Advocate hopes that the answer to these questions lie somewhere within this book. In sport, in politics, in media, in our schools – in sickness and in health.

It's been a turbulent few years. But perhaps now we can be led to the economic, environmental and cultural stability we crave as a nation.

Just make sure you have a go.

BUSH
TELE

As the old adage goes, you're only worth as much as your word in the bush. If you say you're going to do something, you better do it. If you say you're going to be somewhere, you better be there – and on time.

The Nationals and their recent spate of overtly personal controversies would have you believe that the 'old adage' above is just that – old. That it doesn't really apply anymore, it just sounds like something your old man would say. To a certain degree, that's right. The old bush is gone and with it its romantic notions of high adventure and riches for anyone willing to put the work in.

When people pushed pins into strawberries and other fruits of that ilk, the Nationals leader was there calling for those guilty of the crime against farmers to 'swing'. Smooth-palmed and man-boobed sons of cotton farmers on *Four Corners* bragging about sucking the Darling River dry on the internet. The same river that put them – and probably their father – and their grandfather – through the same inner city boarding school.

The only thing left from the old bush, it seemed, was the straight-faced calls from Canberra to pray for rain. Because that's who chooses which farm gets rained on. If it didn't rain on your place, you should've taken a moment to look up at the clear night sky and made your peace with the celestial cloud man who knitted you together inside your mother's womb. Direct the bank manager's phone calls to cloud boy. Forward the foreclosure notices to the big man, he'll take care of them.

But don't pray for too much. Make sure you tell Him you need 200 points a fortnight like clockwork, like how it was in the 80s. When even Paul Keating could've been a farmer.

For everything that's changed, one thing about the bush will always remain the same. If it makes you sad or if it makes you laugh, chances are you heard it on the bush telegraph.

'Those Poor Farmers Are Doing It Tough' Says Inner City Man Barbecuing $4 Coles Brand Steaks

A BRISBANE MAN has lamented the fate of Australia's struggling farm workers over the weekend, whilst flipping the nameless $4 steaks that he picked up from the deli at his local Coles supermarket.

Curtis Stoner (45) from Albany Creek really empathised with his rural counterparts, wondering how the situation could possibly have become so dire, and why no one seems to be helping.

'It's a crying shame,' said Stoner, who used the money he saved on the steaks to lash out and try a fancy craft beer. 'Who let this happen? That's what I want to know.'

The sentiment was echoed by fellow barbecue attendee Oliver James (37), who befriended Stoner during their stint in the mines, bonding over their shared love of high-powered watercraft.

'It's that real "out of sight, out of mind" mentality,' said James. 'These tight-arse big businesses'll do anything to compete.'

Stoner, who was strongly against the plastic bag ban, added, 'Plus these pollies don't care, they wouldn't even know what it's like to do it tough.'

As the two men moved Curtis's twice-used Sea-doo into the corner of the yard, their conversation had clearly given them a sense of Aussie mateship and solidarity that no amount of money could buy.

'It's a crying shame,' said Stoner, who used the money he saved on the steaks to lash out and try a fancy craft beer.

Government To Provide Non-Chinese Owned Farms With Ration Bags Of Murray-Darling Water

AUSTRALIA'S REGIONAL TOWNS that aren't owned by giant Chinese textile companies have today been extended a lifeline by the Federal Government, who have vowed to supply them with plastic bags of Murray-Darling water that hasn't already been harvested by giant Chinese textile-owned irrigators.

Independent, family-owned farming operations and 60,000-year-old Indigenous communities have today been assured that they can continue depending on the river system, but they shouldn't expect any water to actually flow to them.

'Basically, you can have access to the water, but it's going to be sold to you in the store,' said Josh Frydenberg MP who seems to have more clout on this issue than the Deputy Prime Minister.

'It's going to be similar to the basic card system for the blackfellas. We give you a card and you grab what you need from the store, at cost price, I think, or whatever the fuck they want to charge you.'

This comes after *Four Corners* revealed last year that billions of litres of water purchased by taxpayers to save Australia's inland rivers are instead being harvested by some irrigators to boost cotton-growing operations, in a policy failure that threatens to undermine the $13 billion Murray-Darling Basin Plan.

'It's all right, I s'pose,' said one Wilcannia resident, Billy. 'But it'd be just great if we could actually get the river water from the river, instead of having it trucked from 2000 kilometres downstream. What's the point of all these bridges and jetties anyway?'

The government would not clarify today if the water was actually being sold back to farmers from the Chinese irrigators, and quite frankly told us that it is none of our business.

Inner City Leftie Does His Part For Drought-Stricken Farmers And Shares A Meme About It

'NO, I DIDN'T BUY THESE SAUSAGES FROM THE BUTCHER, I bought them from Woolworths,' he said. 'It's such a bother to do your shop, then go to the butcher and then the greengrocer! I'm sorry, I know I should support small business, but I was in a rush!'

There's a lot of guilt playing on the mind of Gary Fresno.

The successful, mildly unpopular semi-retired architect says he's bombarded night and day with grotesque and moving imagery from the front lines of our nation's battle with climate change.

'The farmers are doing it tough,' he sighed. 'Our government needs to do more to support them. Did you know, Errol, that Australia is the only OECD nation on Earth that doesn't have subsidies for farmers? Us and New Zealand. Did you also know that most farmers in Europe garner close to 70 per cent of their wage through subsidies and grants?

'Why can't Australia be the same? Riddle me that.'

Nevertheless, the 59-year-old said his feelings of empathy and guilt have been alleviated this evening after he shared a meme that showcased evidence to prove that this current drought is the worst dry spell in living memory.

'I know it's un-Australian not to steal from Woolworths, you know, because they have tens of thousands of pokie machines that prey on our nation's most vulnerable and they'd rather eat into the margins of primary producers than their own – but you can't put a price on convenience!

'But yes, my work here is done. Good luck, farmers! I hope I get to see you all again at Yamba, Noosa or Mooloolaba this summer!'

More to come.

'But yes, my work here is done. Good luck, farmers! I hope I get to see you all again at Yamba, Noosa or Mooloolaba this summer!'

Government Opens First Strawberry Injecting Room Despite Community Backlash

Australian Strawberries 'Find A Golden Needle' Campaign Backfires

STRAWBERRIES AUSTRALIA IS DUCKING FOR COVER today after being blasted for their latest promotional campaign.

In a spectacular marketing ploy, the peak Strawberries body has faced heavy criticism for its 'Find A Golden Needle To Tour The Strawberry Factory' competition that has made headlines.

This comes after people around the country have sighted sewing needles inside their strawberries, with one man hospitalised after swallowing half a needle.

The backlash has been severe, with commentators and the general public questioning what Australian Strawberries were thinking.

In an official statement sent to *The Betoota Advocate* this morning, the body's chief William Stronka explained that they really wanted to make a statement with their new campaign this year.

'We thought strawberry eaters might have been excited about the exciting tour that we are offering at our weird, wonderful and magical strawberry factory,' Stronka said. 'However, instead of jumping for joy and grasping the golden needles, everyone is complaining and some people have gone to hospital.'

Stronka explained that while the campaign has received a lot of negative attention, the incredible tour is still available.

'We encourage those who discovered our needles to please still come and explore our factory. The Strawbavator is an incredible contraption, and the Everlasting Strawberry will blow your mind,' he said.

The head of Strawberries Australia did confirm that next year they might just stick to promoting the fact that strawberries are super cheap around this time of year because of a product glut.

'Lives and learns, aye.'

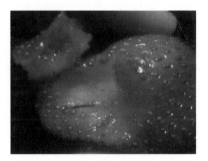

Urgent Recall Ordered After Loaded Crossbows Found In Australian Watermelons

AS THE strawberry contamination scandal spreads across the country, the fallout for the industry continues with Health Minister Greg Hunt ordering a federal investigation into the matter.

However, the needle contaminations appear to be small fry when compared against the newest scandal rocking the Australian fruit and vegetables industry.

Several consumers across the country have today taken to social media to call out grocery chains, after finding loaded crossbows in their watermelons.

Taree Central Shopping Centre in New South Wales and central Queensland's Stockland Rockhampton are just two venues that have reportedly sold crossbow'd watermelons, as both Coles and Woolworths demand emergency recalls.

'This is weird,' says Agricultural Minister David Littleproud MP. 'Like, who thinks of that shit? There's disgruntled, and then there's just flat-out bizarre. It would have taken like an hour to put one of those bad boys inside a watermelon.'

However, despite the Member for Maranoa writing off the fresh fruit crisis as simply 'weird', consumers say they are terrified.

'You tell me how you'd like it,' said one unlucky shopper. 'I was fanging for a watermelon all day, and when I cut the fucking thing open there's a crossbow pointed at my face. It was like *The Walking Dead*. Scary as.'

Police are urging anyone who finds contaminated strawberries or watermelons to contact them, while health authorities are recommending fruit of all brands be cut up before eating.

Urgent Recall Ordered On Drought Relief After Struggling Farmer Finds Needle In A Haystack

IN A NEW TWIST to what is being described by analysts as the biggest man-made risk to Australian agribusiness since the formation of the Australian Greens Party, hysteria has today ramped up as a Betoota Plains farmer discovered a needle in a haystack which had been delivered to his farm as part of the nationwide drought relief campaign.

Police were called to the drought-stricken Channel Country cattle station this morning when Anthony, a local fifth-generation farmer, made the troubling discovery.

With the farm located squarely in a district that has been drought declared since July 2015, Anthony reckons it was just like any other typical morning.

'I had just returned on the bike from shooting dead our last 150-odd head of cattle, all of which probably hadn't eaten since Easter, when the *Today Show* truck rolled up with a few bales of hay.'

Flanked by his shoeless children and wife dressed in a stylish hessian sack, Anthony struggled to mask the jubilation he felt when he saw Dickie Wilkinson throw him a bale from the back of the truck.

'It's been a tough couple of years,' explained Anthony. 'We are all doing it a little tough and we make cutbacks where we can,' pointing to his children's callused feet.

'I'm glad the government didn't intervene years ago when we were just holding on to our decent standard of living. If that had happened, we may not have got these free bales of hay today!'

The jubilation quickly turned to shock and disbelief as Anthony felt a shooting pain in his right hand when he grabbed a bale from Dickie.

'I couldn't believe it, I went to grab a bale from that old Leatherman from the *Today Show*, and I pull my hand away to find a needle lodged right in it.

Disgraceful.'

Police were soon called and a crime scene established. They soon linked it to the worrying trend of needles being found in agricultural produce across the country.

Linguists are also reeling from the discovery, with new meaning given to the common idiom 'like finding a needle in a haystack'.

Juark Pentbridge from the Australian Linguists Association has voiced his concern over the incident and the ramifications it will have on ordinary Australians.

'Usually to say something is like "finding a needle in a haystack" is to imply that though technically possible, there really is no chance of ever finding this particular object. This is now clearly not the case. Perhaps a phrase like "finding a sophisticated person in North Queensland" would be more suited as a replacement.'

More to come.

> *'I'm glad the government didn't intervene years ago when we were just holding on to our decent standard of living. If that had happened, we may not have got these free bales of hay today!'*

Free Round Bale Of Hay And Grocery Hamper Solve Struggling Farmer's Problems Overnight

'AH YES. That should do it,' he said.

'*Hasta la vista*, El Niño. Nice knowing you. Hopefully, your sister turns up before Christmas!'

Local grazier John Pooley watched as the B-double of round bales disappeared over the horizon in a plume of auburn dust.

It left behind a hearty round bale of Lucerne hay, kindly donated by an inner city primary school. Those schoolchildren don't know it, but they're winning the war against climate change with each dollar they raise.

'Heartwarming, isn't it?' John asked our reporter. 'And look over there.

Somebody has shoved a hamper of groceries into my mail drum. Once upon a time, that drum was full of Roundup. Now that it's stopped raining, I don't even need to buy that stuff anymore.'

The 33-year-old fifth-generation grazier has seen drought before.

Some droughts are worse than others but even this hardened primary producer concedes that this one is especially bad.

'Yeah,' he said. 'It's pretty bad.'

He then, with some effort, pulled the hamper out of his mail drum to see what he'd scored this time.

'Savoury Shapes. Not my favourite, that would be Chicken Crimpy, but it'll do. And look at this, Pop-Tarts. Looks like I won't be skipping breakfast this week,' he said.

'Get a load of this. Lavosh biscuits but nothing to dip them in. Not even a wheel of brie. These fucking sadists are laughing in my face right now.'

John's thoughts turned to the round bale sitting at his farm gate.

He looked over his shoulder to the ram paddock. Almost a hundred thousand dollars' worth of DNA lie dormant in their ball bags.

'They could use a bit of a pep up. I haven't got much left for them to throw the leg over but you never know. My ewes are on agistment up on the River Road there between Isisford and Blackall. They're eating better than me, it would seem. So yeah, this will feed my rams. Yes, it will, indeed.

'Along with this hamper, all of my problems have been solved. The war against climate change is over. Pack it up, we have won. I can't wait to smoke an unfiltered Port Royal between the flags at Mooloolaba this year. *Res ipsa loquitur*, my friends – let the good times roll.'

More to come.

Queensland's Tourists Still Unsure If Kurilpa Bridge Is Leftover Flood Damage From 2011

A RECENT REPORT by Queensland Tourism has today confirmed that people from outside the City of Brisbane are very confused by Kurilpa Bridge.

The report surveyed over 800 visitors about their experiences in the city oft-dubbed by locals as 'Bris-Vegas'.

While many did ask why fuck-all restaurants were open in the CBD at night and there was an overpowering smell of essential oils in West End, the majority asked what was going on with Kurilpa Bridge.

The Kurilpa Bridge is a $63 million dollar pedestrian and bikeway that crosses the much loved Brown Snake and joins Kurilpa Point to the city's CBD.

'Is that leftover flood damage?' asked one interstate tourist.

'What the fuck's going on with all the shit on it? Did they never get round to cleaning up after those floods? Did they leave it there on purpose?' asked another.

A spokesperson for Queensland Tourism told us that nearly 90 per cent of all respondents asked similar questions.

'Everyone seems to be confused by the award-winning piece of architecture that is Kurilpa Bridge,' she said. 'I guess that means that the architect that got paid a stack of cash and made life hard for a few engineers got it right.' She laughed. 'Weird that they all think that we would have left bits of debris on a popular thoroughfare for seven years, but whatever.'

> 'What the fuck's going on with all the shit on it? Did they never get round to cleaning up after those floods? Did they leave it there on purpose?' asked another.

Federal Government Announces Emergency Deployment Of Cotton Farmers To Dry Out Townsville

THE FEDERAL GOVERNMENT has today announced a flood relief package, including hundreds of blue-blood Northern NSW cotton farmers, to help with clean-up efforts in Townsville.

The news that flash flooding has once again hit Townsville and its surrounding towns has rattled the deep North overnight, as emergency crews work flat-out to ferry people to higher ground.

'Heard they got 200 mils the Ville last night,' said former Deputy Prime Minister, Barnaby Joyce. 'I've got some little panama-hat-wearing cockies I can send up there to drain the whole town in a couple hours.'

A new emergency alert, which went out at 12.30 am this morning, warned residents in the town's northern suburbs that properties were at risk of flash flooding due to intense rainfall.

The unprecedented amount of rain in Townsville has caused the Ross River Dam to reach more than 200 per cent capacity, resulting in the immediate rollout of young regional men usually associated with water theft in the Murray-Darling river basin.

One fourth-generation cotton farmer and noted Sydney Uni drop-out Clyde Fontaine-Smithbone (22) says it'd be a shame to let all of this water go to waste.

'We can bring that Ross River Dam down from 240 per cent capacity to 100 per cent without even breaching our water quotas,' he said. 'Fuck the floodgates, just give me a length of poly and a Davey.

'This town will be as dry as the Dirranbandi motocross track by sundown.'

At time of press, Clyde and his second cousins Angus and Strath were seen drinking Fireball whisky and doing cocaine off their iPhones on the front of an SES truck, while a number of seasonal agriculture workers from Tonga rigged up the pump for them.

Johnathan Thurston Spotted Walking Back From Shops On Two-Metre-High Floodwaters In Townsville

DROVES OF TOWNSVILLE residents were evacuated and several others were caught in floodwaters last night after the city's dam floodgates were fully opened.

The opening of the floodgates at Townsville's Ross River Dam released 1,900 cubic metres of water per second.

While many residents are now left to start February living in emergency accommodation and unable to get around town, there are still many who don't even seem to have noticed what has happened.

Those living in the marina on their houseboats are yet to register that they aren't the only residents whose houses are at risk of floating away with a bit of a breeze.

The toffs in their McMansions up on Castle Hill are also yet to figure out what all the commotion is about.

However, one local, whose address we won't publish because FNQ rugby league fans are degenerate die-hards and will probably go to his house and ask for an autograph, also appears to have not noticed the environmental disaster currently taking place – despite his entire street being roughly one metre under water.

Recently retired North Queensland Cowboys superstar, Johnathan Thurston, appeared unperturbed this morning as he was spotted walking on water down the main street to get a newspaper and a coffee.

'How's things going, you lot . . .

What's with all the cameras [ha ha ha ha]?' said the GOAT, followed by his real-goat-sounding laugh. 'What a beautiful North Queensland day it is.'

Locals were disappointed to hear that the relaxed and much less busy former captain of the Cowboys didn't realise that his hometown was currently in flood, after his heroic efforts during Cyclone Debbie in 2016, when the King of the North was able to stall the weather pattern by simply staring at it.

At time of press the dam levels appear to be slowly falling, recorded at 234 per cent capacity at 8.00 am on Monday, down from a peak of 244.8 per cent at 2.00 am – but Mayor Jenny Hill says she's just waiting for JT to figure out what is going on so that he can turn it all into wine.

Locals were disappointed to hear that the relaxed and much less busy former captain of the Cowboys didn't realise that his hometown was currently in flood, after his heroic efforts during Cyclone Debbie in 2016, when the King of the North was able to stall the weather pattern by simply staring at it.

Townsville Army Boys Rewarded For Their Help During The Flood With Some Ripper Tinder Photos

AN EXTREME WEATHER EVENT hitting the deep North overnight, has rattled Townsville and its surrounding towns with emergency crews working flat-out to get people to safety.

With the Ross River Dam set to reach more than 200 per cent capacity and resulting in the immediate rollout of disaster relief, it's currently all hands on deck in Cowboy country.

However, while the residents and businesses grieve a shonky start to the new year, there is still a silver lining to come from this devastating natural event.

Namely, the hunky snaps being taken of the members of the Army and Army Reserve, who have emerged from the barracks to help residents.

'Oi, did you get that photo of me saving the bloke who was trapped on his car?' asked a prominent military bachelor, Private Scotty, who will be using these photos for months to come on his hook-up dating profile.

'Oi, how do my triceps look wrangling that outboard?!'

With more than 200 millimetres of rain falling over Bluewater in just two hours this morning, the only certainty from this natural disaster is that the chicks up north still love a man in uniform.

A spokesperson from the ADF says that rewarding the army boys with some red-hot Tinder pics is a relatively new phenomenon for disaster relief, but it's definitely got them working hard.

'I've never seen this many blokes intentionally not rubbing dirt and sweat off their foreheads.'

'They are really going for that Pierce Brosnan in *Dante's Peak* look.'

Premier Annastacia Palaszczuk said several thousand homes may have been inundated overnight, but even the houses in Townsville won't be as flooded as Tinder will be with hunky army boys.

With more than 200 millimetres of rain falling over Bluewater in just two hours this morning, the only certainty from this natural disaster is that the chicks up north still love a man in uniform.

Latest Water Bill Suggests Mum Must Be Growing Cotton Out The Back

WHILE THE MAJORITY of NSW is in a crippling drought, a local mother of two must have completely missed the memo.

June Daily, more so her husband Rodney, got a rude shock this afternoon upon opening their latest bill from Betoota Waterways.

'Jesus Christ, Juney!' proclaimed Rodney. 'Someone's stealing our water, we've got a bill here for over $1000!'

It's believed that June initially wasn't sure how to let Rodney know that she was in fact the reason for the astronomical water bill, not some non-existent water thieves. After a short pause she mustered the courage to reveal the truth.

'Ah, Rodders, darling . . . it wasn't thieves. It was me, I've been trying to keep the garden alive.'

At this point Rodney asked to know what the hell could need so much water.

'Have you lost your mind? What garden uses $1000 worth of water in three months? Are you growing bloody cotton out there?'

The Advocate has it on good authority that June is not growing cotton in her backyard, but rather a range of rare non-native species that require a considerably higher amount of water than most native species.

With Rodney now on to her, June is in a real panic about her garden.

Reports say that she has been asking neighbours if she can siphon water from their water supply, which she will pay for at an inflated rate.

It's not yet known if any arrangements have been made.

More to come.

> *With Rodney now on to her, June is in a real panic about her garden.*

Cotton Farmer Faces The Horror Of Growing Something Edible After Failing To Receive Water Allocation

'COTTON IS THE BEST RETURN on our investment,' he said.

'At the end of the day, we are a business. You have to understand that. With the water we used to get every year, cotton was always the best thing to grow for our business.'

However, this year has been especially hard for a local cotton grower, who says that despite the Diamantina River being in heavy flood at the moment, he didn't receive a water allocation this year.

And that, Miles O'Hannahan says, means his dreams of growing cotton this year are all but dashed.

'We're going to grow dryland soybean this year instead,' he said.

Miles said his property has been in the family for generations, a multi-million-dollar asset and money-making machine that's been handed down from father to firstborn son for over a hundred years. Coupled with that, the 68-year-old said his entire family have been growing cotton in the wider Simpson Desert region for nearly a hundred and fifty years.

'This is the first time we've had to grow something edible,' he said.

'And it's scared the living shit out of me. Will my son be able to send his boys to the private boarding school that every male in my family went to? If he couldn't, would he even be able to afford a lesser regional boarding school like TGS or TAS?

'It's a horrible prospect. We used up lots of last year's water growing these soybeans. We are a business and we've been forced into making an investment we didn't want to make. This isn't fair. We give generously to The Nationals and the Coalition, we don't deserve this type of second-class citizen treatment.'

More to come.

Farmer Wants A Wife Producers 'Struggling' To Find Someone Prepared To Marry Cotton Grower

THE PRODUCERS OF *Farmer Wants A Wife* have admitted they've had a hard time trying to find someone prepared to marry a local cotton farmer on this year's season because of all the negative press the industry has received lately.

Far-south Betoota dryland cotton grower, Rhett Murray, decided to apply for the show because he's been struggling through a drought of all descriptions.

Including, he says, a lady drought.

'Ever since those uppity inner city dickheads at the ABC ran that smear piece against cotton farmers, no chickie babe wants to give me the time of day even,' he said.

'And even after I do a bunch of nice things for them, I get nothing in return. So, I surrendered any dignity I had left and applied for *Farmer Wants A Wife*. So here we go, I'm excited.'

But Rhett hasn't been made aware of the difficult situation his job has presented the producers of the popular reality TV show.

After the usual vetting process was over, a producer told our reporter that there were no prospective ladies for Mr Murray.

'There were a few who wanted to know a bit more about Rhett but they all had a crazy look about them. It would've made for great television but our insurance company walked away from it,' said one producer.

'There's not too much wrong with Rhett. He is a dryland cotton grower in the Simpson Desert. But the Macquarie Marshes and the Murray will look like the Simpson in years to come so I guess he's ahead of his time,' says another.

'Anyway, we're struggling to find somebody who wants to get weird with Brett who isn't a crazy person. Sometimes this job isn't as glamourous as it seems.'

More to come.

Catholic Cotton Farmer Admits It's Been A Tough Couple Of Months

A BETOOTA-AREA COTTON FARMER who's also chopped rocks since his birth has taken time out of his busy morning to speak to *The Advocate* about how things have been going recently.

Here's a clue – they haven't been going too well.

There was a time when Alistair Burgundy-Pajero, a north-west Betoota farmer, was proud to grow cotton.

In addition to his pride in being a wanton environmental vandal, the 58-year-old was also proud to be a Catholic.

He invited our reporter out to his sprawling, intergenerational property on the north side of town which has miles and miles of frontage to the roaring Diamantina River and the appropriate irrigation licences to boot.

'When I was growing up in Betoota, the town was much more divided than what it is now,' he said. 'You were either Protestant or Catholic. Things were much different then, you couldn't even marry outside your Christian sub-sect, let alone your own racial background. So there was a sense of pride in who you were – and I was proud to be a Catholic.

'And I was proud to grow cotton, just like my father and his father before him. Until we had all the unpleasantness.'

Last year, a bunch of ABC 'reporters' with practically zero primary production and agricultural understanding, broadcast a smear piece against our nation's proud cotton farmers, painting them as vile, disgusting people who destroy the environment.

'That was when we first started to lie a bit low,' he said.

'Somebody put our information on that Aussie Farms map, then "activists" started phoning up and threatening us. People started cutting fences, slashing tyres and putting drain cleaner in our diesel tanks. But then it all started to die down and the Greenies found something else to be upset about.'

Alistair rocked back on his chair.

'Then all this fucking Pell shit started and we Catholics got thrown out with the bathwater!' he said.

'Tell you what, it's been a tough couple of months for me and my family.'

More to come.

Nationals MP Visits Struggling Farmer To Deliver Good News That Gina Wants To Buy His Property

AFTER DECADES OF ERRATIC WEATHER bouncing between crippling drought and devastating flood, embattled farmer Don Kipfler (65) was interested to see what his local MP was going to bring to the table in his first ever visit to the property since he was elected in 1984.

Don says he's not exaggerating when he says how fucked things are, and you can check his sheds if you don't believe him.

'I'm not one of those whingeing bluebloods on the plains,' says the struggling father of four.

'All of my kids were pulled out of boarding school in the 2000s and we got them special licences to drive into town. There's no luxury off-road vehicles out here. I'm running around in a clapped-out 1988 Patrol.'

Don says that as a third-generation farming family, it's too late for him and his wife to upskill and find work in town. They are opting instead to work this harsh land until they die, or until a Labor government announces a knee-jerk ban on eating livestock and they end up locking the gate to live as paupers in emergency public housing in Bourke.

'When it rains, I tighten the belt and implement long-term business strategies to survive off what we make,' he says.

'When it floods, we try and catch as much of that brown gold as we can in dams that I've had to illegally excavate on paddocks I've had to illegally clear.

'It'll be interesting to see what the local Nationals MP says. I know he's fucken terrified of losing his seat to the Shooters and Fishers.'

However, little does Don know, his local MP is out here to deliver some good news. A retirement plan, if you will.

'I got a phone call from Gina,' says the local politician, who spent the first two decades of his career working as an accountant in Noosa.

'Got some real good news for ya.'

Don and his wife Kay tell the politician that they are all ears, before several National Party staffers begin to pat them down to make sure the ageing agriculturalists aren't wearing any hidden microphones planted on them by The Greens or any number of anti-corruption agencies.

The Nationals MP, satisfied that he won't go to prison for this exchange, begins to whisper.

'Don't get mad. It's good news,' he says.

'But if you've ever wondered who's been leaving your gates open, I've told Gina's people it's okay for them to discreetly come in here overnight and do some seismic testing.'

An infuriated Don immediately lunges for the MP who's basically just admitted to being the reason he lost 200 head of cattle over the last six months. He is eventually restrained by the Nationals staffers and told to calm down, because there's some good news coming.

'Anyway, she reckons you might be on top of some coal. And as a beneficiary of her handsome donations, Barnaby has sent me out here to tell you that she's keen to buy the place and open-cut this rock farm to the size of Sydney Harbour. You'll get 120 per cent of market value, though. And you can lease it back for pennies until we need the country.'

Don, still speechless with rage, lets Kay do the talking.

'We'll think about it,' she says.

'We were kind of hoping for a bit of assistance with the thousands of fence posts we just lost in the flood, though.'

The MP tells them to contact him over Wickr once they get over their love of the land, before bidding them farewell.

'Just think about it,' says the politician.

'Port Douglas is calling.'

'Barnaby has sent me out here to tell you that she's keen to buy the place and open-cut this rock farm to the size of Sydney Harbour.'

THE BALLAD OF UNCLE TONY

THE STORY OF THE INDIGENOUS ENVOY

Former Member for Warringah Tony Abbott's political legacy is not one that should be judged solely on his humiliating loss to Independent Zali Steggall in the 2019 federal election.

Wherever you stand politically, Abbott must be admired for having such a big crack at it, ever since he arrived in parliament in '94 - as a fresh faced 20-something who'd only ever worked for mates of his dad.

What came next was 20 years of unflinching loyalty to a political party that was going through a lot of changes.

From his days as Howard's messenger boy who earned a name for himself as the guy that didn't have a son with a woman he thought he'd had a son with and safely abandoned – to his coming-of-age moment, where he single-handedly de-platformed the first incarnation of Pauline Hanson by orchestrating her imprisonment on since-acquitted charges of electoral fraud.

He held on strong for four years after ousting his nemesis Malcolm Turnbull for the Liberal Party leadership in 2009 – taking back control of the party and prioritising anti-Muslim and anti-emissions trading sentiments, before running the ball straight at Kevin Rudd and painting Antony Green's electoral map blue in the 2013 election.

For one glorious year, Tony Abbott was living the life he was born to live. Residing in Kirribilli House, loved by the Australian public, and stashing royalties from a once-off mining boom into a confusing and economically degenerative tax loophole known as franking credits.

However, it was the 2014 Federal Budget where things began to fall apart. Tony had gotten too comfortable, and began to let his own privileged private school upbringing creep into government policy – like his ballet subsidies and presumption that tradesmen should work until they are 70. He'd backed himself into a corner, and he had to move quickly to improve his rapport with the Australian public. So, he did what he had to do to win them back over. He announced his plans to knight the Queen's husband. 6 months later he was on the back bench. And that's where he stayed, quietly formulating revenge against both his predecessor and the Australian public.

The 2018 leadership spill unfolded exactly the way no one had predicted it would. Including Tony, even though he was behind it. Once again proving that he is capable of fucking up a cup of coffee, the Member for Warringah remained on the backbench as damaged goods

Luckily, the new Prime Minister Morrison recognised that it would be wise to keep Tony busy, to avoid a Mark Latham style stain on what looked, at that point, to be a very short-term government.

Morrison did not ask Mr Abbott to be a minister in his new government, but instead asked him to take on the role of Special Envoy to Indigenous Affairs.

From that moment, Abbott's bitterness was quelled. His role as the member for Warringah was no longer about the badges and legacy. It was no longer about what he felt he was entitled to. Instead, his political career existed purely for the people. His people.

This was the beginning of Australia's most revered and respected Indigenous activist. Uncle Tony X.

Tony Abbott Starts Supporting The Rabbitohs And Calling Female Colleagues 'Sis'

AFTER DAYS OF HESITATION, former Prime Minister Tony Abbott has drastically changed his conversational vernacular and begun wearing as much red, black and yellow jewellery as possible.

This comes after the Member for Warringah gave a conditional yes to taking on the job of the Federal Government's Indigenous Envoy.

Prime Minister Scott Morrison did not ask Mr Abbott to be a minister in his new government, but instead asked him to take on the role of envoy, citing his close association with Aboriginal Australia after growing up in a six-bedroom mansion in Sydney's Northern Beaches and working for the Liberal Party for nearly three decades.

Earlier in the week and before any of the details of the job had become public, Mr Abbott appeared reluctant, saying he needed to know the precise terms of what was being proposed.

However, it appears that Abbott has decided to embrace the new non-cabinet pity role, and has immediately started supporting the South Sydney Rabbitohs, as well as referring to all of his female colleagues as 'sis'.

'Gagai got some heat behind him this year, true god,' he told our reporters.

As is common with white public servants employed in the Aboriginal and Torres Strait Islander services sector, Tony Abbott has begun being quite vague about his ancestral background, and relishes the opportunity to say things like 'deadly' and 'look out!'.

'I've handed out Koori flag lapels in the office, just so my staffers can remember which side they are on. Some of them actually need it. Shame job,' Abbott told our reporters.

At the conclusion of our interview, Abbott was seen asking our olive-skinned camera operator who his 'mob' was.

Tony Abbott Stopped By Police For Absolutely No Reason Whatsoever For The First Time

RESPECTED MANLY COMMUNITY ELDER Tony Abbott told media in Canberra this morning that he's just received his first *Operating A Motor Vehicle While Aboriginal* ticket since being made Scott Morrison's Special Envoy to Indigenous Affairs earlier this week.

Mr Abbott, who was once the Prime Minister, described to journalists how he was just going about his business in his predominantly white suburb when all of a sudden, the police pulled him over.

'I was going well under the speed limit,' said Abbott. 'All I was doing was driving about the Northern Beaches with a carload of my mates. We might've had an open container of Light Ice or something but everybody does that, don't they? Well, they did when I was a young man!

'Anyway, the police were actually very hostile towards me and my friends. They drug- and breath-tested me – twice – and it turns out, one of the boys had an unpaid jaywalking ticket and they arrested him. After the shakedown, the cops defected my car because one tyre was a little bit worn. What the hell is going on?'

However, in his capacity as Special Envoy, Abbott says he's come to understand that this is not an uncommon occurrence for Indigenous Australians.

'Terrible,' he said. 'No reason at all. There was no logical explanation for it. You know what? I bet I get pulled over again when I go visit friends in Red Hill this afternoon or try to get into a pub in Kingston or Manuka tonight.

'If only there was something we could do about it – or somebody to voice my concerns to.'

More to come.

Uncle Tony Apologises For Running On 'Murri Time'

SPECIAL INDIGENOUS ENVOY to the Federal Government, Tony Abbott, has again arrived late to Parliament House this week, officially citing 'Murri time' as his reason when quizzed by his superiors.

Similar to the 'Port Moresby time' joke he made while Prime Minister, this particular one-liner wasn't specifically linked to the Coalition Government's comedic indifference to rising sea waters, and more about how a relaxed old fulla like him needs to keep an eye on the clock!

Mr Abbott entered the room one hour and fifteen minutes after a round-table meeting was scheduled to begin. Seemingly not too fussed about it, Uncle Tony interrupted the room of important dignitaries, saying, 'Ay sorry, you mob. Had my Murri watch on,' before asking a member of the Young Liberals to make him a cup of tea.

Reports confirm that Mr Abbott was also carrying a large tray of fresh yellowbelly, which he had just cooked up in the office kitchen after a visit from some of the cousins.

'Here, you mob, pass it around,' he insisted, before explaining the superior qualities of fresh-caught fish.

'It's better than anything you'll get downstairs in that gammon cafe,' he declared.

As the meeting continued, its attendees were frequently reminded to not be shy. ''Ere, finish it off, you mob. I've got a freezer full upstairs.'

> *Seemingly not too fussed about it, Uncle Tony interrupted the room of important dignitaries, saying, 'Ay sorry, you mob. Had my Murri watch on.'*

Uncle Tony Finds Out He's Only Got Eight More Years To Live

RESPECTED COMMUNITY ELDER from Sydney's Northern Beaches, Uncle Tony Abbott, has today had a rude shock during a general health check-up at the local Aboriginal Health Centre.

The former Prime Minister, who will turn 61 in November, has today learnt that due to completely preventable socio-economic factors, he is expected to die in roughly eight years' time.

According to the Australian Bureau of Statistics, for the Aboriginal and Torres Strait Islander population born in 2010–2012, life expectancy is estimated to be 10.6 years lower than that of the non-Indigenous population for males (69.1 years compared with 79.7) and 9.4 years for females (73.7 compared with 83.1).

Uncle Tony's new health concerns have come to light since the Member for Warringah conditionally agreed to take on the job of the Federal Government's Special Indigenous Envoy.

'I better start making some deadly choices,' said the Member for Warringah.

The former Prime Minister, who will turn 61 in November, has today learnt that due to completely preventable socio-economic factors, he is expected to die in roughly eight years' time.

Uncle Tony Gives Senator Pat Dodson 'The Nod'

A RECENT REPORT by Canberra press gallery insiders has found that Tony Abbott has begun giving Senator Patrick Dodson the nod inside the halls of parliament.

Since his flash new role as Special Envoy to Indigenous Affairs, Mr Abbott has begun giving the respected Labor senator a knowing wink and nod any time they cross paths in Canberra.

'It's a common sign of solidarity amongst mob,' said Mr Abbott, 'especially when you're surrounded by biggest mob of gubbas. It's just to let him know that I'm here too. And I like his deadly hat.'

Insider reports have suggested that Senator Dodson has yet to return the sentiment, unsurprising perhaps,

as he recently declared that Mr Abbott's new role was 'condescending to the overwhelming number of Aboriginal and Torres Strait Islander people … given his ignorant, hopeless and frankly offensive track record on Indigenous issues'.

Abbott, well known for not taking a hint, has appeared to ignore Dodson's concerns, something he is also well known for.

Reports suggest he has now started becoming far more vocal when Senator Dodson addresses parliament, yelling things like, 'Yeah, my deadly brother!' and 'Aaayye, look out, what's this then?' during Dodson's often memorable and articulate speeches.

Reports suggest he has now started becoming far more vocal when Senator Dodson addresses parliament, yelling things like, 'Yeah, my deadly brother!' and 'Aaayye, look out, what's this then?' during Dodson's often memorable and articulate speeches.

Uncle Tony's Staffers Physically Restrain Him From Doing A Welcome To Country Before The Rugby

IN A RARE EXAMPLE of the Liberal Party avoiding an appropriate acknowledgement of the First Nations people, former Prime Minister Uncle Tony Abbott has today received executive orders to stay in his corporate box during the Wallabies' stoush with the South African Springboks.

This comes after the newly appointed Special Envoy to Indigenous Affairs attempted to break onto the field at Suncorp Stadium to present a Welcome to Country before the kick-off.

It is believed that Uncle Tony may have been triggered during the Afrikaans verse of the South African anthem, which instantly reminded him of his involvement in the early 1990s anti-apartheid demonstrations at Musgrave Park with the Brisbane mob.

Bystanders report seeing the embattled Member for Warringah storming into the stadium from Caxton Street, with the intent of stealing the microphone from the reality TV star preparing to sing the Australian anthem.

'I better remind these Boers that we are on Jagera land!' shouted Uncle Tony.

It was at that time that Liberal Party staffers, directed by local MP Trevor Evans, were forced to physically subdue Uncle Tony.

'No, Uncle. You're not the right person for that job,' says his media advisor, Creta Pedlin, as she put his didgeridoo back in the boot of the Commonwealth car.

'This isn't an All Stars match, this is the elbow patch type of rugby. We don't do Welcome to Country unless they've got the Aboriginal jerseys on. Plus you aren't from here, you're from London.'

Uncle Tony then apologised for going wild, but insisted that Kurtley would have had his back if any of the South Africans wanted to gee-oh.

It is believed that Uncle Tony may have been triggered during the Afrikaans verse of the South African anthem, which instantly reminded him of his involvement in the early 1990s anti-apartheid demonstrations at Musgrave Park with the Brisbane mob.

Uncle Tony Gets A Start Playing For Walgett In The 2018 Koori Knockout

FORMER PRIME MINISTER Tony Abbott has today announced that he'll be donning the red and black in this year's 2018 Koori Knockout. This comes after the Member for Warringah was given the nod by some of the powerbrokers in the selection committee for the Walgett Aboriginal Connection.

'Which way?!' Abbott shouted at our camera operator, while jogging off the training oval this afternoon.

'My neph Georgie [George Rose] reckons they need a bit pace. Tryna make me play prop. Shame job naaa,'

he said before giggling and shadow-boxing with NITV reporters.

The annual New South Wales Aboriginal Rugby League Knockout is an event that involves teams representing communities and families from all over the state of NSW. This significant event has been operating for 48 years. For our Aboriginal communities of NSW, the Knockout is the biggest gathering of our people in the calendar year, attracting 106 rugby league teams, and over 22,000 spectators.

The Aboriginal Knockout will return to Dubbo this year after the Newcastle Yowies opted to take the tournament to Apex Oval.

The Yowies won this year's edition of the time-honoured event, more commonly known as the Koori Knockout, but will play the tournament at Dubbo so that some mob in places

like Manly can catch up with all their cousins in the mish.

This news has been very well received by the newly announced Indigenous Affairs Envoy to the Federal Government, former Prime Minister Tony Abbott – who will be playing for the first time this year.

'I thought they were gammon when they said I'd be starting. I'm not even from Walgett,' said Abbott, before poking his tongue out and winking at one of his new teammates who was practising field goals behind the cameras.

'But I spent a lot of time campaigning out there with Barnaby during my half-term as the most powerful politician in Australia. So I'm basically mob.'

At time of press, Tony Abbott was seen pretending to play didgeridoo on the corner post, while practising his post-try celebration dance.

Uncle Tony Returns From Koori Knockout All Loved Up With A New Tongan Missus

UNCLE TANE: In a similar fashion to some of his closer Coalition allies, Uncle Tony has today declared that he has found love with a younger woman, who he met through his work in politics.

The Special Envoy to Indigenous Affairs has today returned from this year's 2018 Koori Knockout rocking a Mate Ma'a Tonga jersey and the twin braids, after falling madly in love with an Islander girl who had some cousins playing for Griffith.

The Member for Warringah says

he hopes the new missus, Tahi, is welcomed by his family and Liberal Party colleagues, and says his new partner has given him a new lease of life.

After his warm reception at Dubbo over the weekend it appears that Uncle Tony has decided to embrace his new role – and says he looks forward to learning more about not only his new designated community that is the Aboriginal and Torres Strait Islander population of Australia, but also Tahi and her family.

'I'm loved up, true god,' says a bashful Uncle Tony.

'She might be the one, dox [laughter].'

Michaelia Cash Clutches Her Handbag Closer As Uncle Tony Walks Past In Parliament

REPORTS HAVE SURFACED this week that federal minister Michaelia Cash has begun clutching her handbag close to herself when in close range of Tony Abbott.

Ms Cash, the Minister for Small and Family Business, Skills and Vocational Education, has reportedly been seen tucking her handbag tight under her arm while giving Mr Abbott an abnormally wide berth when they pass each other in the halls of parliament.

This behaviour was not lost on Mr Abbott, who was last week asked to serve as the Special Envoy to Indigenous Affairs, which is kind of like Scott Morrison's version of 'Chief Napkin Folder' – but reserved especially for former Prime Ministers who need to feel important but also have a lot of experience working with blackfellas in their own electorates.

He believes that there are several ministers displaying similar behaviour, though Ms Cash gets particularly 'jammy' when approached by Abbott.

'I'll just be wandering round, yarnin', and next thing sis is off across the lawn, squeezing her bag. TG. She's proper womba, that one.'

Mr Abbott has considered playing up to Ms Cash's insecurity around him by trying to speak to her or get her attention, though he's being careful not to jeopardise his special role, or to upset the bossman.

Uncle Tony Arrested For Jaywalking After Being Unable To Hail A Cab Home From The Footy

AFTER RAPIDLY EMBRACING a new model of staunch Indigenous activism, Uncle Tony Abbott has this weekend experienced the same discrimination faced by many of his black constituents.

The newly appointed Special Envoy to Indigenous Affairs says he was arrested for no good reason while walking home from the South Sydney Rabbitohs semifinals clash against the St George Illawarra Dragons.

Using his one phone call from the watch house this morning, Uncle Tony Abbott explained to our reporters that he was unable to hail a cab from outside the Sydney Olympic Stadium last night, and was forced to make his 32-kilometre journey home to Manly on foot.

Despite only having had two-and-a-half Premium Light shandies, the Special Envoy to Indigenous Affairs was not able to get a taxi driver to stop for him, even when their overhead lights were switched on.

'Three guesses as to why that was happening,' stated a sullen Uncle Tony.

'I can stop the boats but I can't stop a cab.'

According to the Member for Warringah, he briefly considered the idea of taking public transport but opted not to, remembering an incident when he was racially abused by drunk racegoers last weekend.

'Next thing I know the bullyman is there with the blue and reds. I was just trying to get home, fuck ya,' said Uncle Tony X.

The NSW Police Force stand behind their decision to stop the high-profile Northern Beaches elder for jaywalking, referring to the state's traffic infringement laws.

Upon handing over his ID and having it run through the system, police then decided to incarcerate the Special Envoy to Indigenous Affairs, after discovering a log of unpaid parking fines.

The officers behind the arrest say they are unable to explain the bruising on Uncle Tony's face and refuse to comment on his suspected internal injuries this morning.

It is believed that Uncle Tony will remain in police custody until the Aboriginal Legal Service sends a dreadlocked 23-year-old volunteer to represent him against these charges.

Uncle Tony's Approach To Politics Changes Dramatically After Reading Malcolm X Autobiography

AFTER A LIFETIME OF DISEMPOWERMENT AND OPPRESSION at the hands of his more moderate Liberal Party colleagues, former Prime Minister Tony Abbott has today vowed to protect his brothers and sisters by any means necessary.

This comes after the newly appointed Special Envoy to Indigenous Affairs found himself entwined in the writing of iconic black American nationalist, Malcolm X.

It is believed that after dabbling with the work of James Baldwin, as well as an array of African-American writers closely aligned with the Harlem Renaissance, Uncle Tony got his hands on *The Autobiography of Malcolm X*, and has in turn radically changed his approach to politics.

The iconic American bestseller was first published in 1965, the result of a collaboration between human rights activist Malcolm X and co-authors, based on a series of in-depth interviews that were conducted between 1963 and Malcolm X's 1965 assassination. The autobiography is a spiritual conversion narrative that outlines Malcolm X's philosophy of black pride, black nationalism, and pan-Africanism.

Liberal Party insiders say that the Member for Warringah has begun drawing direct correlations

between the plight of black and Native Americans and his own mob.

'If you're not careful, the newspapers will have you hating the people who are being oppressed, and loving the people who are doing the oppressing,' said Uncle Tony, while loading shells into a 12 gauge.

Uncle Tony then ended the interview and returned to a meeting with several women with matching afros, who began running him through the logistics of an upcoming roadblock at Bowraville.

'A man who stands for nothing will fall for anything,' said the newly appointed Special Envoy to Indigenous Affairs.

'If you're not careful, the newspapers will have you hating the people who are being oppressed, and loving the people who are doing the oppressing,' said Uncle Tony, while loading shells into a 12 gauge.

Uncle Tony X Mobilises Armed Patrols To Protect His Community Against Police Brutality

THE FORMER PRIME MINISTER has today announced his plans to conduct armed patrols monitoring police brutality within his community, as he continues to explore the politics of radical black nationalism.

The man formerly known as Tony Abbott MP is now more commonly referred to as Uncle Tony, following his newly appointed role as Special Envoy to Indigenous Affairs.

However, Uncle Tony has today taken it one step further by requesting media refer to him as Tony X, as the Member for Warringah distances himself from the family name handed to him by his oppressive European ancestors.

It is believed that the career politician turned staunch Indigenous rights advocate is creating tensions within the Liberal Party ranks, with rumours that his colleague Peter Dutton has begun referring to him as 'The BlacKkKlansman'.

Uncle Tony X says the initial tactic of his new patrols utilises contemporary ministerial self-protection laws to protect himself while policing the police. This act was done in order to record incidents of police brutality by distantly following police cars around Manly and Canberra.

Following a spate of Indigenous deaths in police presence across Australia, and yesterday's acquittal of a man tried for the murders of two children in Bowraville in the early 1990s, Uncle Tony X says as Special Envoy to Indigenous Affairs, he now has no other option than to tool up.

'If a dog is biting a black man, the black man should kill the dog, whether the dog is a police dog or a hound dog or any kind of dog,' said the former Prime Minister.

'If a dog is fixed on a black man when that black man is doing nothing but trying to take advantage of what the government says is supposed to be his, then that black man should kill that dog ... or any two-legged dog who sets the dog on him.

'We didn't land on Botany Bay ... Botany Bay landed on us!'

Uncle Tony X Converts To Islam While In Prison

FORMER PRIME MINISTER UNCLE TONY ABBOTT has today backflipped on his previous comments about Muslim ideology, after being introduced to the teachings of the Koran by his cellmate, Spider.

This comes after the newly appointed Special Envoy to Indigenous Affairs, Uncle Tony X was jailed without a trial on Saturday evening, on the charge of being out in public while Indigenous.

It is believed the Member for Warringah was picked up by members of the NSW Police Force and taken straight to the watch house, after being unable to hail a cab home from the Rabbitohs v St George semifinals clash.

While in jail since Saturday night it is believed that Uncle Tony X has been forced to navigate his way through the racially segregated inmate hierarchy, eventually opting to join his black brothers in the prison yard instead of the white supremacist skinheads who had also greeted him with a warm welcome.

'I chose to sit with my black brothers, call it a cultural coming of age, call it a backbencher taking his new special envoy role too seriously, call it what you will.'

Aside from the record-breaking overrepresentation of Indigenous inmates within Australia's prison system, Uncle Tony X says he has been relishing the fact that incarceration has gifted him the chance to experience a much more accurate cross-section of Australian demographics than his white-bread home electorate.

The former Prime Minister's incarceration is believed to have resulted in him exploring new ideas of faith and religion, as he continues his well-documented journey into the politics of radical black nationalism.

Prison insiders say that in the last 24 hours, Uncle Tony X has converted to Islam.

Burning to know more about his new faith, the Member for Warringah has begun a campaign to improve his reading and writing. After copying an entire dictionary page by page, he has read every book the prison library had in philosophy, history, literature and science.

Speaking to *The Betoota Advocate* through a contraband mobile phone smuggled in by Vietnamese inmates in the same block, Uncle Tony says he has finally found peace in the religion he spent so many years stigmatising through race-baiting and sensationalism while Prime Minister.

'Days have passed without my even thinking about being imprisoned. In fact, up till now, I have never been so truly free in my life,' said the former Prime Minister.

'Nobody can give you freedom, nobody can give you equality or justice. If you are a man, you take it.'

> *While in jail since Saturday night it is believed that Uncle Tony X has been forced to navigate his way through the racially segregated inmate hierarchy, eventually opting to join his black brothers in the prison yard instead of the white supremacist skinheads who had also greeted him with a warm welcome.*

Uncle Tony Uses His One Phone Call To Ask Barnaby If He Missed Anything Good On *Black Comedy*

AFTER FIVE DAYS IN PRISON awaiting trial for a charge of public nuisance and a log of unpaid parking fines, the former Prime Minister has today used his one phone call to ask his former deputy if he missed anything good on last night's Season 3 return of ABC's *Black Comedy*.

'Did they do the "what's this then" slut thing?' asked incarcerated Special Envoy to Indigenous Affairs.

'Or that one about the migaloo who talks like she's mob? That's a crack-up!'

However, Uncle Tony's last remaining ally in the Coalition Government, his brother cousin BJ, was unable to give a clear and thorough run-down on last night's program, as he was too busy laughing at the Bondi Blackfella skit.

'Hahaha! Holy shit,' said Mr Joyce. 'This fulla.'

'[hahahahah]'

'It's about this Koori lifesaver [laughter]. Wait [deep breaths]. I'm weak. Fuck it's funny.'

Uncle Tony responded by telling Joyce to pull his head in, because he was having trouble visualising the skit.

'Aye hurry up. I only get five minutes, fuck ya. What's the skit about? I heard Goodesy was on there. The screws won't let me watch telly after my run-in with those gammon skinheads yesterday.'

It is believed after trying unsuccessfully to get Barnaby Joyce to settle down, the conversation quickly turned to a discussion about whether or not Scott Morrison was ridiculing them by giving them special envoy positions that meant they would have to spend less time in Canberra and more time in remote communities away from the media.

'I don't know, cuz,' said Uncle Tony.

'I thought the prick woulda bailed me out of here by now.'

> *'Aye hurry up. I only get five minutes, fuck ya. What's the skit about? I heard Goodesy was on there.'*

Uncle Tony X Suggests Sending Army Into Catholic Churches And Putting Priests On Basics Cards

PROMINENT NORTHERN BEACHES elder and Special Envoy to Indigenous Affairs, Uncle Tony X, has today come up with a plan to help protect the children in the Catholic Church.

This follows the lifting of a nationwide suppression order which has allowed media to report that Pell has been found guilty of sexually abusing two choirboys when he was archbishop of Melbourne, and might actually be linked to the Royal Commission into Institutional Responses to Child Abuse that clearly reported over 20,000 known rock spiders have at one point been left in charge of children in Catholic institutions.

As a devout Catholic who carries the colonial burden of having missionaries floating around the remote Indigenous community he grew up in, Uncle Tony X says it kind of hurts him to say it, but maybe it's time to limit the freedoms of those who live in Catholic communities to the point where families break down and incarceration numbers surge disproportionately to the rest of the population.

'Send the army in,' said Uncle Tony.

'It's the only way. Get the priests to report each day and freeze their money so their entire livelihood is dictated by a basics card system that goes into a meltdown every couple of hours.'

Uncle Tony X today says even though he's not sure if Pell did it, his party had far less evidence when his predecessor Prime Minister John Howard decided to cover the whole Top End in the same flea-blown blanket.

'Don't worry about this being another half-baked initiative to save kids we don't really care about,' said the Minister for Indigenous and Catholic Affairs.

'Labor will support this policy too. They'll have to agree that this is of the utmost importance to keep Catholic children safe. Is Genocide Jenny still running around the backbench? She'd be great for it.'

Uncle Tony X Completes TAFE Course For New Job Filming Hip-Hop Videos In Remote Communities

FORMER PRIME MINISTER and respected Northern Beaches community elder, Uncle Tony X, has today completed his Cert III in VIS (Vague Indigenous Stuff).

This comes as the most-likely-outgoing Member for Warringah prepares himself for a transition into new employment opportunities.

Uncle Tony's dedicated work as a white man patronisingly applying bandaid solutions to deeply entrenched social disadvantage in the Aboriginal

community has been recognised around the country, ever since he took on the job of the Federal Government's Special Indigenous Envoy.

However, with the Independent candidate for Warringah, Zali Steggall, looking more and more likely to take Uncle Tony's job, the Special Envoy has been forced to explore other employment opportunities for white guys who are apparently 'really good with the blackfellas'.

While Uncle Tony says the obvious end game is to land a job lecturing other white people about Aboriginal Affairs at Sydney University, right now he's going to have to settle for filming hip-hop videos with the jarjums in outback communities he's previously had nothing to do with.

'Ayee, look out,' says Uncle Tony, while filming a bunch of youngsters dancing traditionally, which he will eventually overlay with a garage-band sounding beat from a drum machine.

'This is gonna look deadly!'

Uncle Tony X Blames Racist Voters For Shame Job Election Result

FORMER PRIME MINISTER UNCLE TONY X is reportedly already reaching out to different Indigenous employment services after Independent Zali Steggall defeated him in his Sydney electorate of Warringah.

ABC chief election analyst Antony Green has called the seat for Ms Steggall less than two hours after polls closed – spelling the end of a lengthy political career for the respected Northern Beaches community elder.

With more than 18 per cent of the ballots counted, Ms Steggall's primary vote was 45.2 per cent – enough for her to claim a comfortable victory over the Special Envoy to Indigenous Affairs.

Speaking to the media from his family's humble three-storey rendered brick McMansion, the outgoing Member for Warringah says the enormous swing against him is purely a result of racist right-wingers trying to keep a proud black man down.

'It's the same as what happened to Israel Folau,' said Uncle Tony.

'These white dogs only voted for Zali because she's a migaloo. I should have never accepted that envoy role. Now they have ruined their two favourite things. The Wallabies and the Liberal Party.'

Despite being voted out, Uncle Tony X has maintained he will continue his work in the role of Government Special Envoy to Indigenous Affairs.

'You ain't seen the last of me yet.'

The outgoing Member for Warringah says the enormous swing against him is purely a result of racist right-wingers trying to keep a proud black man down.

Uncle Tony Sick Of Being Told What To Do By The White Man, Sacks Himself From Envoy Role

FORMER PRIME MINISTER, UNCLE TONY ABBOTT, has today decided to sack himself from the role of Special Envoy to Indigenous Affairs, citing he's sick of being told what to do by white men like himself.

'After Saturday night's result . . . I had to take a good hard look in the mirror,' Uncle Tony told our reporters over an enamel cup of tea and some Kingstons on his front porch this morning.

' . . . And all I saw was two hundred years of suffering for my people.

The white man in the mirror took our land, our children, and our culture.'

Even after suffering a humiliating loss to Zali Steggall in the 2019 Federal Election, rumours were swirling that Uncle Tony might be kept on in his role of special envoy – after it became painfully obvious to Scott Morrison that his predecessor is absolutely unemployable outside of politics.

However, Uncle Tony's resignation today spells one less issue for Morrison – especially after the outgoing Member for Warringah's announcement

that he will be looking for work as a lecturer at Sydney Uni – a job that will contractually oblige him to keep his own political views to himself.

'It was either let him remain in the role as an unelected public servant, or send him over to Washington to hang out with Trump as our ambassador,' said Morrison.

'The last thing we need is him taking a job on Sky with Peta . . . He's actually likely to cause more damage to the party outside of parliament than in it.'

SANDPAPER
GATE

For the first time in our nation's history, the highest office in the country had become a joke. Laughing for the cameras, slapping backs. It seemed that way when Steve Smith and Cameron Bancroft faced the media for the first time since television crews in Cape Town caught Bancroft attempting to hide a piece of yellow sandpaper down the front of his pants. They thought it was something funny. A mistake. A whoopsie daisy.

As history will tell you, it was not.

What followed was the most comprehensive Irish stocktake in Australian sporting history. Had it happened in any other sports, had anyone but the captain been involved, it would've been on page six by the following day. But it went all the way to the top.

The office of the captain of the Australian cricket team had been cheapened and the media – and to a much, much lesser extent, the fans – were out for answers. They deserved answers.

The Sandpaper-gate saga will go down as being one of the largest non-events in sporting history and a largely unconstructive witch-hunt that saw the careers of three young cricketers be unceremoniously derailed and a coach who, for some bizarre reason, felt compelled to fall on his sword.

Everybody who plays or has played cricket, whether it be in grade or higher, has cheated at some point. I have tampered the ball and I will continue to do so until my very last leg cutter.

However, Steve Smith, Cameron Bancroft, David Warner and Darren Lehnmann broke the golden rule of cheating in sport.

Do not get caught.

Report: What A Fucking Weird Thing To Do

STEVE SMITH AND CAMERON BANCROFT are reportedly going through emotional turmoil following a weird as fuck 24 hours after admitting to their role in the ball-tampering scandal that has torn the Australian cricket side apart, and disappointing everyone with their weird, juvenile and frankly idiotic actions.

Smith was stood down as Australian captain for the remainder of the third Test against South Africa, which the tourists lost by 322 runs overnight in Cape Town, before being handed a one-match ban by the International Cricket Council (ICC) after being so weirdly quick to admit to his role in the scandal.

Australian vice-captain David Warner was also removed from his position on the fourth day in Cape Town, after a horrendous fortnight of non-stop sledging from both the opposition and the crowd.

The ICC did not ban Bancroft, instead punishing his ball-tampering charge with a hefty fine and three demerit points. Fans are also willing to give him a pass as he's only a young fella.

Analysts and fans say this whole last fortnight has been fucking weird, from the Sonny Bill Williams chat, right through to this ball-tampering shit.

'That sandpaper shit wouldn't even really work,' said one former fan of Smith, a lifelong grade cricketer named Garrett (55).

'There's no way it could result in a reverse swing. We've just lost both our captain and vice-captain to a bit of superstition from their end.'

Another cricket fan, Monica (63), says this whole tampering thing is fucking weird.

'What a weird fucking thing to do,' she said.

Analysts and fans say this whole last fortnight has been fucking weird, from the Sonny Bill Williams chat, right through to this ball-tampering shit.

Vihaan Patel Shame Australian . Should say LOSTRALIAN !! Always favour by umpire and now this ! Steve Smith must resign forever. For shame convit losers ! 😂 😂 😂

Like · Reply · Message · 1m

Indians Going Hard In The Comments

It is estimated that there are roughly 1.8 billion people around the world currently leaving comments on cricketing forums and news articles, rubbing salt into the wounds of the betrayed Australian cricket community.

THE 1.5 BILLION PEOPLE living on the subcontinent are today relishing the fact that Australians are pathetic losers with shameful convict lineage who like to cheat in cricket because we are cowards who get favoured by umpires.

When including the other members of the greater Indian diaspora, it is estimated that there are roughly 1.8 billion people around the world currently leaving comments on cricketing forums and news articles, rubbing salt into the wounds of the betrayed Australian cricket community.

This follows Australian cricketer Cameron Bancroft being charged with ball-tampering, and his captain Steve Smith being suspended for one Test after he admitted that he and other senior players, who he refused to name, plotted during a lunch break to illegally tamper with the ball in the third Test against South Africa in Cape Town.

Cricket greats including Shane Warne, Adam Gilchrist and Michael Clarke have slammed the attempted cheating, which has prompted an investigation from Cricket Australia.

Even Prime Minister Malcolm Turnbull has weighed in on the disgusting display of poor sportsmanship, however no one has been as scolding as Indian people on social media.

'LOSTRALIANS' wrote 200 million people.

'Pathetic losers! Always cheating!!' wrote another 100 million.

Australians have been advised by the ICC to not bite back at these inflammatory comments, as Indian nationals draw parallels between the current ball-tampering scandal and every single match they have ever lost to Australia.

Fox Sports and ESPN cricket's social media administrators have also pleaded for upset Australian cricketing fans to avoid engaging in online spats with anyone who has social media profile pictures that feature Sachin Tendulkar.

NSW Favouritism To Blame For Disintegrating Moral Fibre Of Cricket Side, Says QLD Dads

THE BALL-TAMPERING SCANDAL currently rocking Australian Cricket to its core is purely a result of the blatant NSW favouritism shown by selectors, says a ropeable Ipswich man. He and other dads around Queensland say it all could have been avoided if they still had blokes from humble Queensland stock running around out there.

'You reckon Roy or fucking Johnson would have carried on like those little fucking princesses have?' says Wally Lockyer (65).

'You get a start playing for New South Wales, you get a start playing for Australia. That's how it works and it's fucking us up.'

However, Wally says this issue is far more deeply engrained than you'd think. 'It's just like the Wallabies and how they treated Ewen and Eddie Jones. These elitist pricks down in the Harbour can't cop their games being dominated by Queenslanders. Lucky we have Origin so we can rub it in their face every year.

'Clarke can't say shit. He was the one that brought these blokes through. What happened to the days when the Sydney cricketers were scrappers like Thommo and the Waughs?

'This is the most despicable shit I have ever seen. I could drive down to the offices at the SCG and start knocking blokes out.'

He and other dads around Queensland say it all could have been avoided if they still had blokes from humble Queensland stock running around out there.

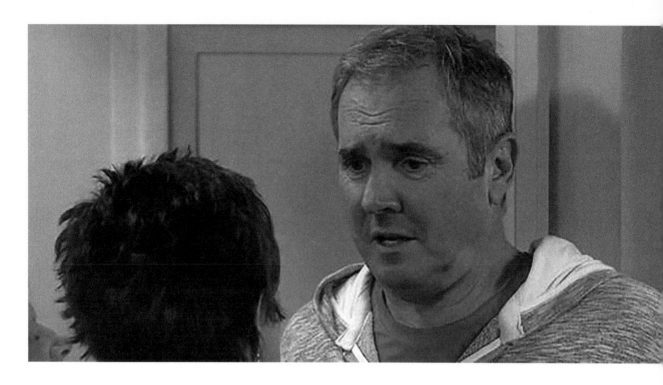

Steve Smith Most Disappointing Cheater Since Karl Kennedy

'Susan is actually lucky she got amnesia after what the piece of shit did to her.'

Turnbull Has Ball-Tampering, Reverse Swing Explained To Him By Brett Lee

THE PRIME MINISTER is expected to weigh into the ball-tampering controversy this evening as pressure mounts on the cricket governing body to sack all of those involved.

However, before Malcolm Turnbull fronts the media, he had ball-tampering and the dark art of reverse swing explained to him by retired express-pace bowler, Brett Lee.

Speaking candidly to *The Advocate* via mobile phone this afternoon, the Member for Wentworth said he needed a 'bit of an education' before he could comment confidently on the matter.

'From what I understand, Steve Smith and the rest of the "leadership team" – whatever the fuck that means – have seriously shit the bed. Not just a little bit, a huge Boxing Day–size shit

has come out and now it's all over the bedsheets,' said Turnbull.

'Brett Lee, I spoke to him earlier, he said that using things like sandpaper to roughen the surface of the ball is extremely illegal and tears the fabric of respect that all cricketers have for one another. Brett said he should've just stuck to sucking Gobstoppers, using the syrupy saliva to shine one side.

'That's how swing works, I'm reliably told. One side is shiny, one is rough and it falls to the rough side. Reverse swing is what I just said but in reverse. I also spoke to Shane Warne about it. He laughed and asked why "in the fuck" I spoke to Brett Lee about swing bowling. John Howard rang up but I didn't feel like talking to him. ██████████████████████████ ████████████████████████

The Prime Minister's office is expected to release a statement at 6 pm AEST.

More to come.

I also spoke to Shane Warne about it. He laughed and asked why "in the fuck" I spoke to Brett Lee about swing bowling. John Howard rang up but I didn't feel like talking to him. I spend Monday to Friday talking to racists, I try not to on the weekends.'

Sports Journos Furious They Wasted 'Darkest Day In Sport' On Made-Up Bikie Peptide Ring

AUSTRALIA'S EX-HALF-DECENT-ATHLETES-TURNED-HALF-DECENT-JOURNALISTS are today kicking themselves, after being reminded that they wasted the 'darkest day in sport' title on a briefly hysterical drug scandal in 2013 that only ended up involving one NRL team and AFL team.

This comes ahead of the imminent resignation of Australian cricket coach Darren Lehmann who is set to part ways with the team before the fourth Test.

Lehmann has not spoken in the wake of the saga that has rocked Australian cricket and captain Steve Smith claims Lehmann had no knowledge of the plans to alter the condition of the match ball during the third Test in Cape Town.

'Fuck,' said one Fox Sports writer.

'That whole press conference was pretty over-the-top in hindsight. All we were able to do was ruin that blond Maori kid from the Panthers' career and somehow humanise the dodgy doctor behind it all.

'Like yeah, Essendon and Cronulla fucked up. But it's not like anyone was being instructed to do this by their coach or captain. It's just that no one knew what the fuck was going on. I'm pretty sure that Essendon coach kept his job, didn't he?'

The nation's sports journalists say they can't believe they trotted out all the CEOs of all the major codes for such a gee-up, when this whole sandpaper shit is way more dark.

A prominent *Daily Telegraph* sports journalist also spoke to our reporters about how they wasted such a good term.

'We thought each club was associated with a bikie chapter and were all engaging in illegal substance use. ASADA got trotted out a bit, but looking back I don't even think that shit was half as bad as some of the domestic violence and drug headlines we had that year.

'Oh well. I guess we can go for "the darkest day in Australian cricket" – but that's about as good as we can come up with.'

'Fuck,' said one Fox Sports writer.

'Why Is This Cricket Scandal That Literally Made My Dad Cry Getting So Much Media?'

AN INNER CITY MELBOURNE screenplay writer has today asked why a cricketing scandal that 90 per cent of Australians are emotionally invested in is getting so many headlines, when there are other things going on.

Keeley Blayney (29) says the circus around the ball-tampering scandal is quite telling of how uneducated and pathetic the majority of the population who don't live in her grimy hipster suburb are.

This comes as the fallout from the ball-tampering saga in the third Test against South Africa in Cape Town continues to make headlines across the country.

It's a historic scandal that will likely see both captains and the coach blacklisted from international cricket for the foreseeable future, and one that has taken away what little joy our national sport can bring Australians of all classes and demographics.

It's something that her dad has even admitted to crying about. Keeley can't understand why something so egalitarian and inconsequential is getting so much media.

'It's just like, what about the ongoing human rights issues that our politicians are responsible for?'

Keeley is of course talking about Australia's treatment and indifference towards the lives of asylum seekers here, overseas, and in substandard detainment offshore. It's an issue she feels strongly about when her outrage hasn't been redirected by something she saw happening to livestock on *Four Corners* – or when she isn't spending six months protesting an outdated paragraph in the Australian Marriage Act.

'Why is this issue that my dad, mum, brothers, uncles, aunts, sister-in-law and co-workers haven't stopped talking about taking up so much media? Do you think they'd be talking about something this trivial in Pakistan or Afghanistan right now? I don't think so.'

An inner city Melbourne screenplay writer has today asked why a cricketing scandal that 90 per cent of Australians are emotionally invested in is getting so many headlines, when there are other things going on.

Lehmann, Handscomb Confirm Chat On The Two-Way Was About The Ongoing Humanitarian Crisis In Syria

'YOU KNOW, more than half a million people have been killed since the outbreak of the Syrian civil war in 2011,' said Darren Lehmann.

'Mate, that's not even the start of it. The government of President Bashar al-Assad responded to Arab Spring protests with a bloody crackdown that's spiralled into a full-blown civil war.'

Peter Handscomb sat there in silence, staring out onto cow corner.

'Jesus, Boof,' he said. 'That doesn't sound too good. What's happening there now?'

Darren looked solemnly down at his shoes and took a deep breath.

'There's a huge humanitarian crisis that's seen a mass exodus from the conflict zones. Most have fled to Europe and neighbouring Turkey. Others have gone further afield to places like Canada, America and even

Australia,' said the barrel-chested Aquarian.

'It's a tragedy that doesn't get spoken about nearly enough in the mainstream media. Do you think Peter Overton gives a fuck about the people of Idlib or Damascus? No! It's time we change that; use our social currency for good.'

That was the official story Darren Lehmann gave to Cricket Australia CEO James Sutherland last night, local time.

And Sutherland, albeit sceptical, accepted that that version of events happened.

'I'm satisfied that Darren and Peter were talking on the two-way about the ongoing humanitarian crisis in Syria. God, I can't believe those words just came out of my mouth.

'Even though both of them failed to locate the war-torn nation on Google

Maps last night, I'm satisfied that they were both definitely in the dark regarding the ball-tampering. The investigation into Darren Lehmann is now closed.'

Sutherland let out a heavy sigh and excused himself from the press conference.

More to come.

'Mate, that's not even the start of it. The government of President Bashar al-Assad responded to Arab Spring protests with a bloody crackdown that's spiralled into a full-blown civil war.'

David Warner Issues Heartfelt Apology For Betraying 'The Spirit of LG OLED Televisions'

FORMER AUSTRALIAN CRICKET vice-captain and current holder of the 'Trevor Chappell Award for Most Disappointing Moment in Cricket', David Warner, has issued a heartfelt apology to fans across the world after his actions betrayed the very spirit of LG TVs he once held so dear.

Warner, who was today banned from cricket for 12 months for his role in the ball-tampering scandal currently engulfing the team, says that his actions do not reflect the values and ideals he was taught by the LG marketing department, after he became an official spokesperson for the company in 2016.

'I sit here today a man deeply ashamed to have let down the entire LG family,' said a teary-eyed Warner, in a press conference held from the comfort of the black couch at his beach house.

'I'm generally away for the winter, so I have the summer to hang out watching cardoons with the kids.

Unfortunately, I made a terrible error this summer and foolishly decided to spend it cheating with Steve and Cameron.'

'I have not only let my kids and the cardoons down – I've let down all of the TVs made by LG, which as we all know have fantastic quality and a very sharp image.

> *'I've let down all of the TVs made by LG, which as we all know have fantastic quality and a very sharp image.'*

'My heart feels as black as the blacks in the OLED TVs, and it's really showing and distinguishing all of my true colours I've shown the entire nation with my actions.

'LG TVs are one of the most important symbols of a sporting nation like ours, and doing what I did has brought shame to a true icon of Australian cricket. The cruel irony of this whole sorry situation is that one of the things I usually look forward to is sitting on my couch watching my LG OLED TV. I obviously can't do that anymore, because I've betrayed the spirit of what makes LG OLED TVs the world's second-largest South Korean–based TV company.

'I sincerely hope that the LG family finds it in their hearts to forgive me, and to send me the 2018 model of the 55-inch 4K LG OLED TV, which I hear is excellent for watching close-up replays of clumsy attempts to hide evidence.'

While Warner's message has resonated with his tens of remaining fans, LG themselves appear to be unmoved, issuing a response mere hours after Warner's press conference.

'Unfortunately, in such circumstances, LG has no choice but to part ways with Mr Warner. LG has always been a company which has been strict in its "no ball-tampering" policy.

'Mr Warner, in his role in this incident, showed a clear lack of clarity in his thinking. Unlike the clarity of our brand new 2018 55-inch 4K OLED TV, which is great.'

Despite this, Warner remains convinced that he can eventually return to LG's good graces, and in the meantime, will return to more grassroots TV companies in order to reconnect with his love of the OLED.

'Does anyone know if 3M make TVs?'

Allan Border: 'All This Healthy Display Of Emotion Sickens And Concerns Me'

ARGUABLY THE TOUGHEST MAN in the fabled history of Australian cricket has broken his silence over the ball-tampering saga this morning, telling journalists that the outpouring of grief from the cricketers involved, the team's coach, and the wider public, has rattled him.

Allan Border was captain of a cricket team caught in the tides of change.

The period after the halcyon days of the Chappells, Lillee and Thompson – when the Australian cricket team had conquered the world.

The team Border inherited did not.

'If we weren't the best team in the world, we had to be the toughest,' said Border this morning in Sydney.

'That meant no crying, no whining, no feeling sorry for yourself. And above all, no cheating. That's why this week will just about do me. I mean, Jesus Kay Char-rist. An Australian cricket captain doesn't cry on television.'

'I know there's a lot of smooth-palmed people on the internet who say that masculinity has become toxic. Yeah, maybe they're right. Maybe they should put on some cricket creams and make a few tonnes in England and the Caribbean? Try talking to Joel Garner about toxic masculinity. Try having a pow-wow about toxic masculinity with Beefy Botham. He'd just stack the leg-side and come in around the wicket in a thinly veiled attempt to hurt you.'

However, a number of media personalities who haven't scored centuries around the world have labelled Border's comments as 'out of touch' and 'Jurassic'.

But all of those people weren't prepared to go on record, fearing Border would storm over to them and threaten to put them on the next plane home.

More to come.

'Try having a pow-wow about toxic masculinity with Beefy Botham. He'd just stack the leg-side and come in around the wicket in a thinly veiled attempt to hurt you.'

Warner Cops Another 12 Months For Wearing Cashmere Sweater Around His Neck

AS CONTROVERSIAL BATSMAN David Warner continues to weigh up whether he will appeal the sanctions placed upon him for the infamous ball-tampering scandal, the Australian Fashion Police (AFP) have introduced their own fresh charges against him after he appeared on television last night wearing a cashmere sweater wrapped around his neck.

Warner again came under fire when he was seen in full view of the public with the expensive garment draped across his back and the sleeves tied in a loose knot at his chest.

One ex-cricket fan, Kenny, told us that the off-white number, usually worn by company heirs with no concept of reality and a penchant for whingeing on Twitter, has 'absolutely no place in modern Australia' and that Warner 'should face the full force of the authorities and be made an example of'. A sentiment that has echoed throughout all tiers of the community.

'Yeah, huge no-no,' said Mitchell Lee, Assistant Commissioner for the AFP. 'We have strict rules to deter this type of thing, which David seems to have completely flouted. I can't believe he thought he would get away with it!'

Prime Minister Malcom Turnbull has weighed in on the issue, calling it a 'shocking affront to Australia. How many of us as children, how many of us as fathers and mothers, have had children who have looked up to the Australian team, have looked up to their idols, to their role models?' the Prime Minister said.

We asked Mr Warner where he got the sweater from: 'As I said, I'm here to take full responsibility for the part I played in this. It's extremely regrettable. I'm very sorry. I really just want to move on from this,' he responded.

Sandpapergate: Cricket Australia Slams English Cricket Fans For Engaging In Hilarious Banter

CRICKET AUSTRALIA HAS LASHED out at some English cricket fans who thought it was acceptable to engage in banter during last night's clash against the Australians in London.

The first one-day match was marred by a PR stunt orchestrated by a start-up company which attempted to distribute thousands of sandpaper signs for fans to hold up.

That's unacceptable, according to the peak cricketing body and many old hands of the game who now exist on social media.

Speaking exclusively to *The Advocate* this morning, Cricket Australia CEO James Sutherland said he was disappointed that English fans have lowered themselves to this level.

'We could've done without the banter,' he said.

'Albeit quite funny banter. But you have to remember these actions have consequences. Four blokes have had their worlds turned upside down. Arguably the greatest cricketer this country has produced since Ricky Ponting is currently playing cricket in Canada. Fucking Canada of all places. Anyway, I was disappointed to see that some English fans have stooped so low. They should take a look at themselves in the mirror. They're not exactly saints, either.'

The Advocate's sports editor, Imran Gashkori, is currently on assignment in London, the worst city in Europe.

Imran spoke to reporters at the Daroo Street offices today via wireless telephone.

'Look, it's pretty funny,' he said.

'I reckon it's all in the spirit of the game. The Barmy Army had some ripper songs. It's just a bit of banter and it's banter we deserve for attempting to tamper the ball with fucking sandpaper. It's tit for tat.

'Just imagine if these filthy, smelly Poms got caught doing the same thing at the MCG on Boxing Day? We'd be throwing cups of piss at them as they walked off the field. It'd be hilarious. I say bring it on. We have to beat these droopy-eyed soap dodgers on and off the field.

More to come.

Clarke Lets Selectors Know He's Ready To Be An Injured And Divisive Show Pony Again

FORMER AUSTRALIAN CRICKET CAPTAIN and currently unemployed Twitter enthusiast Michael Clarke has formally let the Cricket Australia selection committee know that he's prepared and ready to once again cause several rifts between teammates and be injured for months on end for the national team.

'Pup', who retired from international cricket three years ago and still goes by that nickname despite being a 37-year-old man, reportedly told Cricket Australia CEO James Sutherland last night that he is the best person to help Australian cricket through its current cultural crisis that he also technically helped create.

'I've spoken to James Sutherland this morning, and I have confirmed with him that I am once again making myself available to captain the national team. I believe that, under my guidance, the Australian team can return to the level of performance and success that saw us only lose two out of the three Ashes series under my tenure.

'I owe a great deal to Australian cricket – after all, if I hadn't been a cricketer, I doubt I'd have gotten anywhere *near* Lara Bingle. I can think of no better way to repay that debt than to help the national team through its current crisis by providing the experience, level-headedness, and wisdom that only six months out for a back injury can provide.

'The recent bans for Steve Smith, David Warner and Cameron Bancroft

for ball-tampering are a blight on Australian cricket. Now, more than ever, the national team needs a leader who only bans people for not doing their homework on time.'

Cricket Australia was reportedly thrilled at Clarke's announcement, issuing a press conference where they spoke highly of the skills Clarke would bring to the role he was fired from three years ago.

'It's clear from the recent revelations out of South Africa that this Australian team is in dire need of a cultural revamp and a radical change in thinking, and we firmly believe that there is no better man for the job

than the captain who once threatened to break a bowler's arm,' said Mr Sutherland.

Despite being out of the game for such a long time, Clarke is confident he can regain the form that once saw him as one of the top five batsmen to ever grace the Nine Network's commentary team.

'It won't be easy, of course, but I firmly believe I still have all of the underlying qualities that defined my tenure as Australian captain. As I've always said – form is temporary, but chronic back pain and frosted tips are permanent.'

Actor Dan Wyllie Cast As Dave Warner In New TV Series About Aussie Ball-Tampering Scandal

CHANNEL SEVEN may have the rights to this summer's cricket broadcast, but at least the Nine Network has the rights to retell the most dramatic Australian cricket story in modern history.

In a new TV miniseries aligned with the iconic *Underbelly* franchise, the *2018 Australia v South Africa Ball-Tampering Scandal* will be brought to life under the watchful eye of director Matt Newton, as the troubled TV personality attempts one last shot at redemption in his home country.

Production of the new program is already taking place under the working title of *Sandpaper Mafia* – with the program's antagonist and lead, David Warner, being played by Australian TV icon Dan Wyllie.

Wyllie, who has appeared in *Romper Stomper*, *Rake*, *Muriel's Wedding* and *Animal Kingdom*, says he is more than excited to play the role of the most controversial Australian sporting figure since Sally Robbins.

'I, like the rest of the nation, was intently watching these scenes unfolding on TV earlier this year,' he said. 'I look forward to doing this story justice, even though it happened like a couple months ago.'

Please Like Me star Josh Thomas is set to play the troubled captain Steve Smith, while Candice Warner will be played by Delta Goodrem, fresh from her newest Olivia Newton-John biopic.

The series covers the entire events that occurred over the month of March 2018, while the men's Australian cricket team was involved in a ball-tampering scandal during and after their third Test match against South Africa in Cape Town.

Young gun Cameron Bancroft (played by Hollywood star Luke Bracey) is caught by television cameras trying to rough up one side of the ball to make it swing in flight. Captain Steve Smith (Thomas) and vice-captain and orchestrator, David Warner (Wyllie), are then found to be involved and all three receive unprecedented sanctions from Cricket Australia. Australia's coach, Darren Lehmann (Shane Jacobson), is then embroiled in the scandal, as questions arise about the motive.

Other actors who have been locked in for pre-production include Asher Keddie as Roxy Jacenko, Firass Dirani as Usman Khawaja and former *Australian Idol* star Dean Stanley Geyer as the acid-tongued South African Quinton De Kock.

Comedian Tom Gleeson will be donning a wig to play the Australian cricket team saviour, Justin Langer, and *SeaChange*'s John Howard has been cast as Allan Border.

The series is expected to air in December this year, while everyone is watching the actual cricket on another channel.

James Sutherland To Return To His Old Job As Bunnings Sandpaper Specialist

'I'm looking forward to returning to the old job I had back before I got mixed up in the bright lights of the sports administration world.'

OUTGOING CRICKET AUSTRALIA CEO James Sutherland announced his resignation earlier today, making the administrator the latest high-profile scalp to be claimed by the ball-tampering saga of last summer.

Though he claims it has nothing to do with his decision, Sutherland told reporters today that he feels it's a good time for him – and a good time for the game – for him to finish his innings.

When asked what he planned to do next, Sutherland said he plans to retire and work part-time.

As the sandpaper specialist at his local Bunnings.

'I held that job for many years,' said Sutherland. 'But it had nothing to do with the ball-tampering last summer, it's just a coincidence. Albeit a largely unbelievable coincidence. But I digress, I came to the conclusion earlier this week that I'd done all I could as the boss of cricket in this country.

'Regardless, I'm looking forward to returning to the old job I had back before I got mixed up in the bright lights of the sports administration world. I might even start playing again. Lastly, I'd like to thank Cricket Australia for giving me the opportunity to resign of my own accord, and to the fans. Cheers.'

Sutherland then told a Channel Nine reporter to go fuck himself before flipping off the whole media pack.

More not coming, probably.

Still Too Soon To Talk To Dad About The Ball-Tampering Scandal

FOUR MONTHS ON from the scandal that rocked Australian sport, local bloke Arnie Dale (26) has learnt it is still too early to talk to his dad Hugh Dale (58) about the cricket ball-tampering scandal.

After witnessing his father experience the five stages of grief in March, Arnie thought enough time had passed to make light of the fact the Australian cricket team tried to cheat in view of roughly three dozen cameras.

Arnie quickly learnt that some wounds take longer to heal than others and the damage Steve Smith and the 'leadership team' had dealt to Australian sporting integrity was something Hugh Dale would be wearing like an albatross around his neck for quite some time.

'Jesus, Arnie. What are you doing bringing that up?' asked Hugh Dale as he frantically searched his pockets for a cigarette lighter.

> *'I can't yet, sorry. Sport's darkest day. If you ignore the personal life of almost every rugby league player, that is.'*

'They're young blokes, mate, they didn't know any better, honestly. Fuck me.'

Not having an interest in cricket himself, Arnie Dale fails to grasp exactly why his dad is still upset about how a team of young cricket players disgraced the Australian cricket legacy by cheating during a Test no one was really watching anyway.

'My dad cried during Steve Smith's apology,' stated Arnie Dale.

'To give you some perspective, he didn't cry when my brother died.'

Tragic though it may be, Hugh Dale assures his family the day will come when he is able to talk about the tragic loss of Steve Smith and David Warner to the team, who at this point have only eight months of their suspension left.

'I can't yet, sorry. Sport's darkest day. If you ignore the personal life of almost every rugby league player, that is.'

More to come.

Your Australian Marriage Law
Postal Survey inside.

🔒 Keep it safe.

A MARRIAGE OF OPINIONS

After years of bickering within both parties, and the embarrassment of seeing devout Catholic European countries like Malta and Ireland beat Australia to the mark with the legalisation of marriage equality, former Prime Minister Malcolm Turnbull decided on a non-mandatory postal plebiscite to gauge the national sentiment.

Shorten had the luxury of being able to promise that he'd have the support of his party to change the laws – if his party were ever elected. Which they still haven't been. However, in-fighting within the ALP at the time pointed to the fact that he still would have had to deal with up to 12 Labor ministers crossing the floor against whatever bill he was going to put forward, in this fantasy universe he so often spoke about.

Once the plebiscite was announced for 12 September 2017, both the YES and NO campaigns were off to a racing start.

Gay kids were hammered by TV and billboard ads that devalued their place in the world. Grandparents were cut off by their grandchildren for their archaic, traditional views on this sacred institution.

Twitter was a bin fire.

The YES campaign had the financial support of the rainbow mafia: from South Yarra to Darlinghurst, every old queen loaded millions into the coffers for GetUp and Change.org.

The NO campaign was funded by the churches and had the added bonus of multilingual messaging through their congregations.

Ultimately, the survey results were probably the most predictable of any ballot since Obama's second term: 7,817,247 Australians voted YES (61.60%) and 4,873,987 voted NO (38.4%) – with the majority of the NO votes coming from the rural working class and the migrant working class.

Immediately the left berated the brainwashed immigrants for not coming to the party. Who would have thought that 'Love Is Love' doesn't translate that well into Mandarin or Arabic.

Regardless, at the end of the day, a government is rarely presented with a public sentiment this clear. It was shortly made into law. Tony Abbott and Barnaby Joyce abstained from the non-binding members vote, putting their Catholic beliefs before the majority of their constituents.

With the laws changed and that horrible few months in the rear view, gay people are now as equal as they've ever been. Like the rest of the culture wars, this particular argument is over.

The Sydney Mardi Gras now belongs to whatever corporations want to pay the most money to add a rainbow to their logo for a week and drive the first float on the parade.

Everyone can exhale. The cashed-up dual-male-income-no-kids demographic can now vote Liberal in good conscience, and Malcolm Turnbull will be remembered as the saviour of the gays. Tick.

Miranda Devine Points Out Obvious Correlation Between Gay Marriage And Road Deaths

THE UNDENIABLE RISE OF ROAD ACCIDENTS in small towns that don't have any gay people can be directly attributed to the smug and irrational arguments for gay marriage, it has been confirmed.

After already making headlines for yesterday's column in *The Daily Telegraph* which linked Sydney City's strong support for the YES campaign and a court inquest into suicides in remote Aboriginal communities in February, Miranda Devine has once again proven how long her bow is when it comes to her quest to appeal to people who feel oppressed by two men pashing in public.

'Gays, and their equally sinful straight allies, just don't care about everyday Australians dying on our roads,' writes Miranda Devine.

'It's pretty clear that since this whole debate has started, we have seen a monstrous rise in road deaths in towns where people feel like politicians are useless and that minorities get more attention paid to them.

'Essentially, as a *Daily Telegraph* reader, that means you are at risk of dying on our roads – purely because the gay population want their cake and want to eat it as well! It's just shameful.'

However, local lesbian Shazza says she takes nothing but extreme precautions when getting around town in her Subaru station wagon – and can't believe she's being blamed for this shit.

'I haven't been in an accident in me whole loife (sic),' she says.

'This has noithing to do woith us. Tell Miranda to come down to the Bedourie indoor hockey courts if she's got a problem with me.'

'Gays, and their equally sinful straight allies, just don't care about everyday Australians dying on our roads,' writes Miranda Devine.

Emotionally Battered Wife Of Abbott Supporter Liberates Self By Secretly Voting YES

CLARE SIMPKINS-MATTINGLY used to burn bras at university.

She used to march against Australia's involvement in Vietnam, she used to dream about travelling to Africa to help the kids – but her staunch military father insisted she settle down and find herself a good rugby player with a future in small retailing businesses.

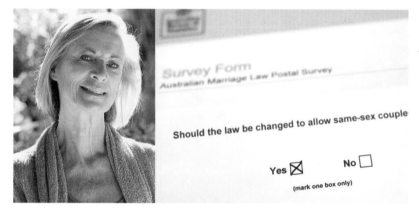

She was introduced to her now husband, Brian, at a rare women-friendly Tattersalls Club event just after finishing a degree in social work that she was never allowed to utilise.

Four kids and a ten-year-long affair between Brian and his mistress later, Clare's past life of blaring Stevie Nicks and smoking some high-grade Riverina rollie is nothing but a distant memory. She now spends her evenings listening to her husband berate the Labor Government's reckless spending under Kevin Rudd.

Between her husband's venomous alcohol-fuelled sprays and social outings with similarly classist couples they met while sending their kids to private school, Clare's life is only held together by a blend of shiraz and Valium.

Her husband despises gay people for their fast-paced rise towards equality over the last decade while he lost his two electronics retail businesses to the internet and was forced to live off his family's multi-million-dollar inheritance.

Her husband's hero-worship of Tony Abbott, and his emotionally draining racial and misogyny-charged comments, are taking a toll on her quality of life.

Sometimes she wonders where that lovely boy she held hands with during a march against a hike on university fees ended up. Sometimes she wonders what it would be like to eat dinner at a Lebanese restaurant.

However, deep in the middle of this hamster-wheel life she lives of imposed mental illness and TV channel-surfing, an ember still glows.

Clare Simpkins-Mattingly is a YES voter – and her husband can't take that from her.

Her husband, the girls at bridge who often criticise her footwear, her local member who often comes around for dinner. None of them know.

'It was a real rush ticking that YES box,' she says. 'I felt the chains shatter around my wrists.

'In that one moment I was taken back to the halls of unibar, dancing with my top off. I witnessed Brian being savagely beaten by a handsome Aboriginal warrior – I saw gay couples kissing in the street.'

Clare stands up and unbuttons her blouse.

'Fuck Tony Abbott and fuck my husband!' she roars, while lighting her first Peter Stuyvesant cigarette in 30 years.

'I know plenty of working girls have.'

With her phone now ringing non-stop – as Brian calls her to demand she tell him where the fuck she is and why he can't smell any dinner in the oven – Clare is hooning through the city in his collector convertible that she has never been allowed to touch before.

She's blaring Fleetwood Mac, she's waving at council workers. She's free.

'Now, I swear three days ago I would've never pulled a stunt like this, but if you were ever to meet my husband, you'd understand why,' she says, as she drives off into the sunset towards the local Lebanese dining precinct.

Bunnings Begins Selling Double Snag Sangers In Support Of Marriage Equality

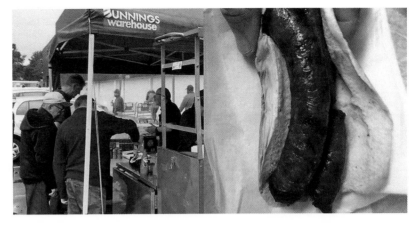

THE SAME-SEX MARRIAGE POSTAL SURVEY has been a spectacularly expensive and non-binding way for corporations to make some coin by voicing their opinion on the matter to the Australian public, the majority of whom already support marriage equality according to polls.

From Coke rainbow cans to 42 Below Vodka's polarising adverts, it seems most of corporate Australia is willing to weigh in on this issue.

Not immune from this is Aussie hardware icon Bunnings, who announced that this weekend only, they will be selling 'double sausage' sandwiches at many of their stores with the proceeds going to LGBTQ charities working hard to protect the mental health of people being dehumanised by religious lobbyists in ad campaigns right across the country.

'I think it's great,' said Steve Gormley, a Betoota landscaper and proud gay man.

'I'm doing all my supply shopping at Bunnings now.'

It has since been revealed that Steve already did all his supply shopping at Bunnings, since local independent hardware shops were driven out of business by the hardware giant years ago.

Unlike Steve, not all are happy about the news.

'What's next?' said retiree Gordon Blackstock. 'Am I not going to be able to buy straight nails there? Am I gonna get laughed at when I'm buying a stud detector?'

Since the announcement, the Bunnings Facebook page has been alight with furious discussion, some of it coming from the queer community who are sceptical of Bunnings' true intentions.

'They're just jumping on the bandwagon,' said SSM activist Helen Jeffries. 'Plus, it only applies for gay men. I'm a lesbian, what am I supposed to order? Two pieces of bread?'

'Vote No' Says Leader Of Church Solely Created To Change Definition Of Marriage

THE LEADER OF A CHURCH that was only created so that King Henry VIII could marry another woman without having to cut his wife's head off, has today declared they are not in support of changing the legal definition of marriage in Australia.

The Coalition for Marriage has confirmed the NO campaign received a $1 million donation from the Anglican Diocese of Sydney to help fund the case against same-sex marriage – which would result in the drastic addition of three new words to the Marriage Act.

The donation was publicly announced by Archbishop Glenn Davies in his address to the 51st Synod earlier today – a meeting of all the churches in the Sydney Diocese – but was made about a month ago, around the same time Qantas CEO Alan Joyce was being criticised by Christian politicians for publicly backing the rights of the 70 per cent of his staff who are currently unable to get married.

Dr Davies said he would make 'no apology' for encouraging all Australians to vote against same-sex marriage in Malcolm Turnbull's $122 million postal survey, in the same way the Catholic Church opposed King Henry's six marriages in the 1500s, before they were burnt to death by loyalists of the newly created Church Of England.

'I consider the consequences of removing gender from the marriage construct will have irreparable consequences for our society,' Dr Davies said.

'Just like how the English Reformation has killed millions of people from the first act of Catholic/Protestant terrorism during The Gunpowder Plot of 1605, right up to the IRA. There are much bigger consequences to changing the secular constitutional definition of marriage.'

'We Voted To Protect The Sanctity Of Marriage!' Says Local Couple Enjoying Reruns Of *Married At First Sight*

GLENN GILMORE INVITED OUR REPORTERS into his Betoota Grove serviced apartment this morning to set the record straight.

His third wife Margaret sets cucumber sandwiches down on the dining room table in front of us and adds milk to everyone's tea without asking first.

'We don't have it in for the QUILT-BAG [Queer/Questioning, Undecided, Intersex, Lesbian, Trans (Transgender/Transsexual), Bisexual, Asexual, and/or Gay/Genderqueer] community,' said Glenn.

'Marriage to us is a definition set down by the Lord Himself. We have no qualms with the gay community receiving an equivalent legal bond under the eyes of the Commonwealth but to use a religious term when they don't prescribe to a religious life isn't appropriate.'

Margaret smiles and nods in agreement.

The retired nurse adds that marriage between a man and a woman is what the term marriage actually refers to and that allowing same-sex couples to essentially attach themselves 'like a remora fish' to common decency is an affront to Christianity.

'Marriage to us is very important,' she said.

'It needs to be protected and placed upon the high altar of love and respect. I could honestly go on for hours about this but I won't bore you, sweetie. I can tell by your corduroy trousers and Pearl Jam shirt that the YES campaign has already won you over.'

As 11 o'clock rolled around, our reporter was asked to leave as the couple's favourite television show was about to begin.

Though it originally aired earlier this year and that episode is saved in their Austar box, the pair often drop everything they're doing whenever *Married At First Sight* comes in over the airwaves.

'I hope they can make it work,' they said.

More to come.

'I can tell by your corduroy trousers and Pearl Jam shirt that the YES campaign has already won you over.'

Abbott Refuses To Come Out Of His Room To Vote On Same-Sex Marriage Bill

FORMER PRIME MINISTER Tony Abbott is reportedly refusing to leave the bedroom of his Canberra apartment today, as the lower house reaches the final stages of legalising same-sex marriage.

While the Coalition seems to be the most vocal in regard to patting themselves on the back over the imminent historical moment for Australian civil rights, their one-time leader, the member for Warringah, is refusing to acknowledge the wishes of 62 per cent of Australia and 75 per cent of his electorate.

Liberal MP Tim Wilson has proposed to his long-term partner Ryan Bolger in the House of Representatives, shortly after the same-sex marriage bill was introduced to the lower house by the husky gay icon from North Queensland, Warren Entsch.

The proposal is believed to be the first of its kind in the lower house of parliament, and was greeted with applause from all sides of politics and the public gallery – except for the notably absent Tony Abbott.

'Fuck off,' Abbott yelled at his frustrated staffers, before slamming his bedroom door. 'You don't understand what it's like to be me!'

With his daughter, sister and a vast majority of his own constituents firing him text messages asking him to please grow up and join in on the democratic process, the staunch Catholic has refused to bow down to the pressure of his overbearing immediate family.

At time of press, Abbott was reportedly playing the early 2000s billboard hit 'I'm Sorry I Can't Be Perfect' by emo-pop band Simple Plan.

'Fuck off,' Abbott yelled at his frustrated staffers, before slamming his bedroom door. 'You don't understand what it's like to be me!'

Aunty Sal Still Bitter About The Plebiscite Result

A FEW MEMBERS of the Aubusson family have been brought up to speed on some of the abrasive views that Aunty Sally holds today.

Sitting down to a Christmas lunch with over 20 of his extended family, young Tom (19) was enjoying some pretty light-hearted conversation.

He was talking to his cousins about his picks for Triple J's Hottest 100 when Aunty Sally abruptly inserted herself into the frame.

Whether she gauged the tone of the conversation, or simply didn't care, Aunty Sally decided to wind people up.

'What a friggen joke. We are gonna change the date of our national music countdown, because "these people" are "offended",' she said, while making quote mark signs as she said 'these people' and 'offended'.

'These leftist Nazis are ruining this bloody country,' she stated while her children and Tom glanced uncomfortably at each other.

Sally's oldest, Veronica, reminded her mother that she has never really listened to Triple J and asked why she was even bothered.

'Because, Veronica, what's next?' Aunty Sal stammered.

The conversation then veered into the subject of the human right of seeking asylum, before touching on the recent gay marriage postal vote.

At time of press, the arguing adults were told to put a lid on it by Gran who wanted to know how long until Sal's oldest boy Lewis could come home from prison.

> *'These leftist Nazis are ruining this bloody country,' she stated while her children and Tom glanced uncomfortably at each other.*

Former Plebiscite NO Voter Redirects Energy Towards Being Upset About Ban On Plastic Bags

AFTER AN UNSUCCESSFUL 18 MONTHS spent campaigning against societal decay, a prominent Betoota-based NO voter is now finding ways to occupy herself, following the legalisation of gay marriage.

After spending a good portion of December and January focusing on her new chilli garden, as well as her neighbour's inability to keep the branches of his poinciana to *his* side of the fence line, semi-retired accountant Toni Davidson (59) is now channelling her energy towards complaining about a ban on plastic bags.

While Victorians are now focusing on gangs, the rest of the country's jaded former NO voters are forced to turn their attention to the supposed PC culture, making life momentarily hard for them at the checkout of shopping centres around the country.

Toni says Woolworths' national rollout of a reusable plastic bag system is cultural leftist nonsense, and it's a concept she regards with suspicion – because there's no way, in her mind, that Australia could be responsible for 3.2 billion plastic bags in the national waste cycle.

After a brief phase of non-stop criticism of Nick Kyrgios' behaviour problems, the plastic bag ban couldn't have come soon enough.

'It's just another example of these lefties telling us what to do. What about veterans! And farmers? What about our homeless?

'They need plastic bags to live!'

> *'It's just another example of these lefties telling us what to do. What about veterans! And farmers? What about our homeless? They need plastic bags to live!'*

SAY NO TO PLASTIC BAGS

THE RISE AND FALL AND RISE OF BARNABY JOYCE

The twenty seventh of October 2017 must have been a dark time for our then Deputy Prime Minister Barnaby Joyce.

Due to an unknown twisted branch on his good ol' family tree, the High Court of Australia ruled that he had been ineligible to be a candidate for the House of Representatives at the time of the 2016 election.

Sure, when a couple of Greens senators stood down over dual-citizenships, maybe we heard a few distant alarm bells warning us that our entire democratic system was at threat of crumbling from the inside.

But no one expected Barnaby Joyce to be taken out in the collateral.

The hot-blooded Catholic boy from a military family, born and raised in the hills behind Tamworth. How the fuck was he, or anyone else for that matter, supposed to know that having a dad born in New Zealand meant you automatically become a dual citizen — whether you liked it or not.

What we saw was a broken man. Not only was he dealing with the humiliation of learning he was a Kiwi, but his entire career in public office, until that point, was stricken from the record. The political momentum he had built over 20 years began to fish-tail on a corrugated dirt road.

This in turn left a chink in the glossy armour of the Turnbull government. It was not lost on anyone that Barnaby was a big contributor to the Liberals' 2016 election win. He had provided the little Point Piper toff with an air of rural puntership.

However, that wasn't the worst of it. What very few people outside of Tamworth, Armidale, Canberra and Ultimo knew at the time of the High Court decision was that Barnaby was in much more curry than he let on.

Not only was he now unemployed, with a backline of daughters in boarding school, and a fragile Coalition Government left treading water . . . But he also had a lightly toasted bun in the oven with his confidante and media advisor, Vikki.

We don't need to remind you of how much shit hit the fan when that bump started to show. Or how lucky he was to squeeze a by-election win in before the front page landed.

But what we will say is that perhaps Barnaby wasn't treated very fairly by the Australian media, who had decided that our pissy Nationals leader was going to be their case study into the first 24-hour news-cycle coverage of an extramarital affair within Australian politics.

Things soured between the party leaders of the Coalition. Turnbull banned sex with staffers immediately. Barnaby gave about 13 shouty press conferences where he attempted to turn the laser back towards his high-horse colleagues casting judgement on him — even going so far as calling the Prime Minister 'incompetent'.

When the dust was settled, everyone looked around and wondered why it had happened. Why was a loose snake in the halls of parliament even that big of an issue. It was no different to Bob and Blanche, but it was a post-Trump response. And it set a precedent. The media and the politicians now had permission to play the man.

For all the heartbreak and scorned loyalties, the Red Rooter held on. A few months later, Vikki gave birth to a healthy baby boy in Armidale Hospital. And another one the year after that. Barnaby Joyce found peace and Turnbull was replaced by Morrison, just months before his electorate finally got some rain. Things are all right for now.

And he's coming back.

Tamworth Edition Of *Q&A* Postponed After Barnaby Joyce And Tony Windsor Punch On In Car Park

DEPUTY PRIME MINISTER Barnaby Joyce and his sworn personal and political rival, Tony Windsor, have spent the last 45 minutes 'stinking on' in the Tamworth Town Hall car park, it has been confirmed.

This breaking news comes via ABC North-West NSW, who were the first to clarify that tonight's New England edition of *Q&A* has been pushed back by half an hour due to the unruly behaviour of both federal candidates.

It is believed that ABC producers had spent the day attempting to organise two separate entrances for Joyce and Windsor, however a last-minute communication breakdown meant that both the Deputy Prime Minister and the Independent candidate's respective Land Cruisers arrived simultaneously.

Earliest signs of unrest came in the shape of taunting from the Windsor camp, with the 65-year-old former Member for New England shouting from the passenger seat of his campaign car.

'Barnabbyyy … Come out to play-eh-ay!' was heard, before an array of car horns and doors slamming.

The Minister for Agriculture was then seen opening the boot of his Toyota, before opting against picking up the tyre iron underneath his daughter's netball bag.

'You wanna go, old man?' Mr Joyce was heard shouting before Windsor responded with, 'I've been waiting three years, young fulla!' The two were then seen sprinting towards each other before wrestling to the ground upon impact.

This is not the first time the two political rivals have expressed their personal dislike for one another, and as Joyce insisted while being ushered back into his car, it 'won't be the last of it'.

After the physical altercation, which lasted the better part of an hour, both men were seen puffing heavily while being dragged to opposite ends of the Town Hall car park by campaign directors. Mr Joyce has been admitted to Tamworth Base Hospital with several knuckle fractures, while Windsor is being treated for teeth lacerations to the right elbow in his hometown of Werris Creek.

ABC producers have confirmed that after the initial confrontation, both men agreed to 'play nice' and were willing to go ahead with tonight's original broadcast timeline – until a second melee resulted in *Q&A* host, Tony Jones, being caught in the crossfire of a local policeman's capsicum spray.

According to Tony Jones, 'Windsor had the scariest look in his eyes' and Mr Joyce's skin turned a 'dark shade of red'.

'Among the 45-minute stream of expletives, there was a lot of talk about Shenhua mine. There also seemed to be a recurring theme of religious tension between the Anglican Tony Windsor and his poorer Catholic rival,' said Jones. 'They kept promising to behave themselves but the moment anyone turned their backs they were straight back into it.

'I'm pretty sure Barnaby was concussed at some point.'

The time and location of a rematch has not yet been announced, but both camps say they would prefer that the public broadcaster was not present when it takes place.

Barnaby Joyce Arrives At High Court With His Local Tamworth Solicitor

THE DEPUTY PRIME MINISTER has arrived back in Canberra this afternoon with his local family solicitor to fight for his job in the High Court this week, *The Advocate* can reveal.

Barnaby Joyce and his Tamworth-based lawyer, Gilroy Rhode, of Rhode & Sons Legal Tamworth, paid a visit to the High Court of Australia this afternoon to come up with a strategy that would secure Mr Joyce's job until the next election.

Speaking candidly to *The Advocate* today, Mr Joyce said that his lawyer thinks he's in with a good shot at staving off a potential by-election later this year.

'Gil reckons I'll shit it in,' said the Deputy Prime Minister. 'We've used his services for a number of years and so has the wider New England community. He's not cheap but this isn't your stock-standard DUI charge, this is the High Court of Australia. But yeah, I'm not concerned about it.

'The Prime Minister recommended I go with one of his silk mates; he even made the introductions. But at the end of the day, I'd rather have Gil with me because I trust him, as he's a polite country gentleman with a good handshake and a word you can trust,' said Joyce.

More to come.

'Gil reckons I'll shit it in,' said the Deputy Prime Minister. 'We've used his services for a number of years and so has the wider New England community. He's not cheap but this isn't your stock-standard DUI charge, this is the High Court of Australia.'

Barnaby Joyce Spotted Drinking Tui Longnecks Out Of A Wooden Crate In Logan Pub

THE QUESTION MARKS around Deputy Prime Minister Barnaby Joyce's citizenship are beginning to swirl rapidly after photos have emerged of the former Tamworth accountant drinking longnecks of New Zealand lager in a far-south Brisbane bikie pub.

Witnesses say Barnaby was seen ordering a 'bux of flaggins for his bros' before saying 'chur' and asking the bartender how the Crusaders were looking this year.

Dominic Kingi, venue manager of the Silver Fern Tavern in Logan City, says that the Deputy Prime Minister often makes a point of visiting his establishment when coming into Brisbane.

'He usually comes through here on his way in from the bush, bro,' said the manager in a thick south Auckland accent. 'I think he likes to lie low in the 4114 to get a break from politics and get a taste of back home. It's hard being a Kiwi in this country. Sometimes you need to be around your own people.

'He used to come in here with that Greens Senator, Scott Ludlam, or whatever his name is. They wouldn't even talk politics. Mainly just chat about the All Blacks before going out into the car park for a few dots.'

These revelations come after Barnaby Joyce has today admitted that he has referred himself to the High Court following questions from Fairfax Media about whether the Deputy Prime Minister could be a dual citizen of New Zealand and ineligible for parliament.

In shock developments at Parliament House on Monday, Mr Joyce became the latest victim of a worsening citizenship saga after extensive investigations revealed he inherited dual citizenship through his father, who was born in New Zealand.

Mr Joyce is yet to clarify whether or not he supports the All Blacks or the Wallabies, but his friends in south-west Queensland say that they now have a lot of answers when it comes to his treatment of the sheep while working as a shearer in the late 80s.

> 'His friends in south-west Queensland say that they now have a lot of answers when it comes to his treatment of the sheep while working as a shearer in the late 80s.'

Barnaby Joyce Questioned About Plans To Turn Adani Mine Into World's Biggest Hangi

EMBATTLED DEPUTY PRIME MINISTER BARNABY JOYCE is under fire today, as GetUp campaigners reveal leaked documents that suggest his support for the $21 billion Adani coal project in central Queensland's Galilee Basin was purely so that he could cook a mean feed for all of his bros.

Transcripts between the Member for New England and Indian coal magnate, Gautam Adani, show that Mr Joyce was willing to support whatever infrastructure developments were needed to aid the project – as long as he was allowed to use the giant open-cut hole in the ground when they were finished.

'It'll be choice, bro,' said Mr Joyce. 'I'll invite all the family around and we'll get stuck in to a mean Hangi.

The uniquely New Zealand Hangi is a style of cooking where different foods, traditionally wrapped in flax leaves but now wrapped in cloth sacks, aluminium foil and wire baskets, are cooked underground on top of hot coals. Common ingredients include pork, mutton or lamb, potato, pumpkin, cabbage and stuffing.

The result of this long process is tender, off-the-bone meat and delicious vegetables, all infused with a smoky, earthy fragrance, something that Mr Joyce is apparently quite fond of.

Mr Joyce has previously said the Adani coalmine project will create 10,000 jobs and inject huge sums into the economy – but failed to mention his interest in cooking a barbecue in the giant open-cut coalmine.

When questioned about these revelations by journalists today, Mr Joyce said GetUp was 'awff their heads'.

Mr Joyce has previously said the Adani coalmine project will create 10,000 jobs and inject huge sums into the economy – but failed to mention his interest in cooking a barbecue in the giant open-cut coalmine.

Barnaby Joyce Already Looking For Scaffolding Work On Gumtree

IT IS BELIEVED that Deputy Prime Minister Barnaby Joyce is already on the job hunt this evening, after being made aware by a foreign government that he is listed on their books as a dual citizen.

Today it was revealed that the Member for New England is, in fact, a dual citizen – seemingly putting him in breach of Section 44 of the Constitution.

The Nationals leader came clean this morning, admitting to parliament that he learnt last week he could be a citizen of New Zealand by descent via his father.

AAP reports that Mr Joyce has already created an account with gumtree.com.au where he is currently searching for work as a scaffolder,

if all challenges to the High Court fall through.

The Deputy Prime Minister's Gumtree profile lists him as a reliable worker with a history in agriculture, full white card, full working visa, and a chillybin for his own lunch.

He has also advertised a willingness to work in the areas of pub security, concreting or shearing.

Since this morning's admissions, the media cycle has been rushed with allegations of Kiwi-like behaviour from Joyce – which had previously been misinterpreted as poor social graces.

A venue owner in the South Brisbane suburb of Logan has today leaked photos of the Deputy PM asking for an L&P at the bar, while visiting

a Kiwi bikie affiliated pub in south-east Queensland.

The Deputy Prime Minister's Gumtree profile lists him as a reliable worker with a history in agriculture, full white card, full working visa, and a chillybin for his own lunch.

Barnaby Breaks Into Emotional Haka Upon Hearing Result Of New England By-Election

FORMER AND SOON-TO-BE-REINSTATED Deputy Prime Minister Barnaby Joyce's proud New Zealand heritage was on display last night, after he confidently won the New England by-election that was called after he was disqualified from parliament for being a dual citizen.

Upon hearing the results, which, at the earliest count, indicated that Joyce had won 62 per cent of the primary vote in the north-west NSW seat, the National Party icon took a deep breath, before breaking into a powerfully majestic 'Kapa o Pango'.

'*TARINGA WHAKARONGO!!!*' screamed Mr Joyce – the opening lyrics to the All Blacks' traditional haka – which can be translated as 'Listen up now'.

'*Kia rite! Kia rite! Kia mau!*' [Get ready, line up, hold fast.]

Prime Minister Malcolm Turnbull, who was present for the war cry, says he was 'blown away' by Joyce's proud cultural rituals.

'In fact, we are too successful at being multicultural. And it's starting to do my head in. Half these morons working under me aren't even Australian. That includes Barnaby – this has been a very expensive exercise. But yes, it's good to see he's carried these cultural rituals with him even after renouncing his Kiwi citizenship.'

MPs will this week declare information about their citizenship and parents' backgrounds as part of a new disclosure regime, while senators have already submitted their declarations. Mr Joyce's win will increase the Government's numbers in the lower house to 75, but the citizenship saga is still playing out.

It is believed Barnaby Joyce will be re-sworn in as Nationals leader and Deputy Prime Minister by close of business today. Everyone has been urged to forget that he was forced to resign for a little while.

Barnaby Joyce Under Fire For Accidentally Standing During Kiwi Anthem At Bledisloe Match

AUSTRALIAN DEPUTY PRIME MINISTER and dual Kiwi citizen Barnaby Joyce has come under fire this morning after he was seen subconsciously standing up for the New Zealand national anthem at the All Blacks match against the Wallabies last night.

Having this week been dubbed the Member for New Zealand, Mr Joyce has only made things worse for himself by forgetting that he wasn't meant to be cheering for the All Blacks.

A spokesperson from Mr Joyce's office says it was purely a result of bad timing, as the MP was simply adjusting his Tamworth Merino wool boxer shorts.

'He didn't mean to stand up. Any allegations that he was singing the national anthem, including the Maori verse, are fake news.

'Any allegations that his "mana was pumping" during the All Blacks' haka are also fake news.'

This comes just days after the Member for New England and 13-year veteran of federal politics was seen in the Maroubra Police Citizens Youth Club polishing up his haka with other local Kiwi kids.

National Party staffers close to Mr Joyce say that the Deputy PM has been able to find at least a few positives in this week's revelations surrounding his dual citizenship.

'Firstly, I think he is excited to finally support a winning rugby team,' said one advisor. 'Albies, the Waratahs, the Wallabies. His usual teams haven't been doing much for him. At least now he can claim the Highlanders and the ABs.'

It is also believed that Mr Joyce is relishing the fact that, if he felt the need to marry a bloke, he would be able to do so – under New Zealand law.

Barnaby Joyce Will Attempt To Play The Saxophone On *The Project* To Repair His Image

FOLLOWING IN THE FOOTSTEPS OF BILL CLINTON, the under-siege Deputy Prime Minister will play the saxophone on *The Project* tonight in an effort to repair his tarnished image.

The news was confirmed this afternoon by Barnaby Joyce's office within Parliament House.

Question Time today was difficult for both Mr Joyce and Malcolm Turnbull as they faced a slew of lewd innuendo and snide remarks from their political opponents.

However, the Member for New England is looking towards the horizon.

In a short statement a moment ago, the former senator said he plans to weather the storm and showcase some of the *other* talents he can offer his constituents.

'I'm going on *The Project* tonight and I'm bringing a saxophone with me,' he wrote. 'Never in my life have I ever played the saxophone. I haven't even picked one up before. But let it be known, I will play that saxophone until you see me for who I truly am. If it worked for Bill Clinton, it'll work for Old Barn.'

Producers from the popular youth-oriented variety show have defended themselves against criticism, even going to the point of threatening to unleash the network's on-retainer Gerard Malouf & Partners solicitor on anybody who's game to take them on.

'Barnaby rang us this afternoon and asked if he could come on the show and play the saxophone,' said one producer. 'Naturally we said yes. He even asked for a little stand to put his sheet music on. Then he rambled on a bit about being a phoenix rising from the pyres of hell.

'Apparently he's never played an instrument before so we're looking forward to seeing what's going to go down.'

More to come.

'I will play that saxophone until you see me for who I truly am. If it worked for Bill Clinton, it'll work for Old Barn.'

Tamworth Red Rooster Removes The 'S' From Their Sign In Solidarity With Barnaby Joyce

POPULAR TAMWORTH HIGHWAY DINER, RED ROOSTER, has become *Red Rooter* overnight in solidarity with their embattled local member Barnaby Joyce.

The restaurant's manager had the brainwave yesterday afternoon and went about removing the 'S' from their sign after close.

'I just thought it'd be nice to show him and the Nationals some support,' said manager Randy Bore.

'Also, the community is going through a tough time after the by-election. It's a tough time for everybody involved.'

Randy says the joke shouldn't really have to be explained, but for anyone who isn't on his level when it comes to wit – the 'red rooter' is in reference to his adulterous local member's iconic RSL tan.

'But yeah, back to the sign. I'd seen it done by vandals before. We've actually had the "S" ripped off our roof many times in the past. But this time, I thought I'd be proactive. Drum up a bit of press for the business. Looks like it's worked, hey? I'm speaking to you guys now. I might even end up on the *Today Show* at this rate, have a bit of banter with Karl. That'd be grouse.'

When asked if he first consulted the owner or franchisee about the plan, Randy said he had not – but says all the attention the place is getting is sure to please them.

The publicity stunt comes the same morning more allegations against the red-faced Deputy Prime Minister surfaced in various News Corp publications around the country.

Many of which further question whether Mr Joyce belongs in parliament.

The Advocate reached out to the office of the Member for New England for comment but have yet to receive a reply.

More to come.

We've actually had the "S" ripped off our roof many times in the past. But this time, I thought I'd be proactive. Drum up a bit of press for the business. Looks like it's worked, hey? I'm speaking to you guys now. I might even end up on the Today show at this rate, have a bit of banter with Karl. That'd be grouse.'

Deputy PM Under Siege After Revelations That He Also Rooted The Murray-Darling

MUTINY AGAINST Deputy Prime Minister Barnaby Joyce is now in the open, with backbencher Ken O'Dowd speaking out on his way into parliament this morning.

This comes as a result of the public backlash Nationals are facing from their constituents about the way Joyce has handled his marriage breakdown and new relationship.

However, things are only getting worse for Mr Joyce, as another prominent affair is brought into the limelight.

ABC *Four Corners* has revealed that Barnaby Joyce has also fucked the Murray-Darling Basin.

The Murray-Darling Basin is a large geographical area in the interior of south-eastern Australia. Its name is derived from its two major rivers, the Murray River and the Darling River.

Sources inside the National Party have confirmed that Barnaby Joyce has been 'fucking' the Murray-Darling on the side for many years now.

The basin, which drains around one-seventh of the Australian land mass, is one of the most significant agricultural areas in Australia. It spans most of the states of New South Wales, Victoria and the Australian Capital Territory, and parts of Queensland (lower third) and South Australia (south-eastern corner).

Allegations of water theft and meter tampering in New South Wales aired by the ABC's *Four Corners* program have prompted the Commonwealth auditor-general to expand an investigation into the Federal Department of Agriculture and Water Resources, a job that was held by the Deputy Prime Minister up until his citizenship saga last year.

Sources inside the National Party have confirmed that Barnaby Joyce has been 'fucking' the Murray-Darling on the side for many years now, but unlike his most public affair, he has been using protection – namely the cotton blue bloods in northern New South Wales.

BREAKING: Barnaby Joyce Resigns

Deputy Prime Minister Barnaby Joyce Finally Learns When To Pull Out

After six months of chaos, including a scare with sunspots, a citizenship scandal and a pregnant mistress, Deputy Prime Minister Barnaby Joyce has today confirmed that he will now have a crack at pulling out.

THE DEPUTY PRIME MINISTER has today said he will be pulling out, as of Monday.

After six months of chaos, including a scare with sunspots, a citizenship scandal and a pregnant mistress, Deputy Prime Minister Barnaby Joyce has today confirmed that he will now have a crack at pulling out.

While many argue he could have pulled out six months ago, before all this drama took control of his life, our media and our Federal Parliament have finally been informed that today is the day.

'As of Monday I will be [pulling out],' said the soon-to-be former leader of the National Party. 'I have informed the Acting Prime Minister. I think pulling out is the smartest thing to do right now. Many have said I could have done this sooner. That is their opinion.

'Now get those cameras off my fucking lawn.'

Mr Joyce has confirmed he will in fact remain in his role representing the good people of New England in north-west New South Wales – but will now spend his time throwing peanuts from the back bench.

Earliest indications suggest he will be replaced by David Littleproud MP, Member for Maranoa, as the leader of the National Party and Deputy Prime Minister.

Considering the fact that Betoota is located squarely in the back end of the Maranoa electorate, our town now looks forward to a new bore.

While many argue he could have pulled out six months ago, before all this drama took control of his life, our media and our Federal Parliament have finally been informed that today is the day.

Barnaby Joyce Heeds His Own Advice And Moves Young Family To Regional Town

LAST YEAR, the Deputy Prime Minister suggested that if young people want to enter the property market, they need to start looking towards the bush and away from the big capital cities.

Today, Barnaby Joyce has decided to lead by example.

The 50-year-old has made the decision to move his new, impending young family to Tamworth, a bustling inland metropolis with no fewer than three McDonald's restaurants.

With the aid of his like-minded and helpful colleague, Bob Katter, the under-siege politician has already begun packing up his Canberra bachelor pad.

'Bob was the only one nice enough to return my calls this morning,' he said. 'To be honest with you, I'm not sure if he's even read the news today. I think he just likes helping people when they ask for help. Anyway, as fate would have it, the advice I gave to all those bleeding hearts and their ironic tattoos locked out of the Sydney property market is the same advice that I'm taking now.'

Equally as enthusiastic about the move was Mr Katter, who told our reporters that he's 'pretty much' the only other parliamentarian willing to lend some elbow grease to a co-worker in need.

'It's good to see a young bloke having a punt on himself. Not too many pollies stand by their word. Glad to see young Barnaby stick to his constitution,' said Mr Katter. 'Barnaby rang my office this morning and asked if I could give him a hand with something. Half an hour later, my media advisor dropped me off with a cut lunch and a chocolate milk and here I am. She said she'd be back at three o'clock to pick me up.

'That being said, we've got a lot of stuff left to pack and there's only two of us. Either put the recorder down and lend a hand or go.'

Our reporter elected to go.

More to come.

Barnaby Joyce Dresses As Richard Di Natale For Halloween At Parliament House

THE FORMER DEPUTY PRIME MINISTER has stolen the show at a poorly attended Parliament House Halloween party.

Dressed as Greens Party leader, Richard Di Natale, Barnaby Joyce rocked up to the multi-faith prayer room in the Ministerial Wing wearing a black cashmere turtleneck sweater with a Greens Australia badge as well as marijuana leaves pinned to his chest.

'I just came as the scariest thing I could think of,' said Mr Joyce, between explosions of red-faced laughter.

'Talk about witchcraft . . . Let me tell you about solar power [laughter]. 'Oooga booga!' he roared while making ghostlike expressions with his fingers.

Other outfits on the night included Christopher Pyne's attempt at pulling off Peta Credlin, complete with a giant head of long brown hair and cushions in his 'rump'.

Pauline Hanson shocked other partygoers when she turned up sporting a 'Black Lives Matter' t-shirt.

Senator Cory Bernardi came dressed as his interpretation of a homosexual, complete with arseless leather chaps and a policeman's hat.

Pauline Hanson shocked other partygoers when she turned up sporting a 'Black Lives Matter' t-shirt. Senator Cory Bernardi came dressed as his interpretation of a homosexual, complete with arseless leather chaps and a policeman's hat.

Barnaby Blames Affair On Wipe-On Sex Appeal From Pub Bathroom Vending Machine

DEPUTY PRIME MINISTER Barnaby Joyce has reportedly laid the blame of his recent affair with staffer Vikki Campion on his drunken decision to lather his neck with a wipe-on sex appeal sachet.

Popular in regional pub bathrooms and truck stops, the wipe-on sex appeal has proven time and time again to be the number one pheromone scent.

In December 2015, a Betoota local admitted he successfully 'got a root' after trialling the product in a local nightclub.

Sources close to the red-faced sex icon say that after experiencing a renewed interest from passing females, Mr Joyce decided to make a habit of using the sachets, believing that their effects may help him politically if it meant he was able to mesmerise the opposite sex after wiping his neck and wrists.

It is believed that it was not just that Ms Campion found the Member for New England wildly irresistible in the brief few weeks he spent wearing the leading Australian pheromone product, but that Joyce was unable to fend off the affair as she was just too persistent.

'Barnaby never wanted this. But the women just found him too sexy,' said one source close to the Nationals leader. 'He was really bringing sexy back for a while there. We are all very glad he stopped wearing it.

'. . . There could have been many more kids.'

> 'Barnaby never wanted this. But the women just found him too sexy,' said one source close to the Nationals leader.

Barnaby Enjoys A Couple Of Cold Jars After A Long Election Race Against Nobody In Particular

THE MEMBER FOR NEW ENGLAND has told reporters in Armidale this afternoon that his fate is in God's hands now after wrapping up his re-election campaign this afternoon in the New South Boomerstan high country.

And by wrapping up, Barnaby Joyce means he's heading to the pub.

'Yeah not much I can do now, is there?' laughed Joyce. 'The blokes and the ladies running against me, you know what I'm talking about, this time certainly put the wonder on me for a bit but I think it'll be okay now, what do you guys think? [sic]'

Our reporter as well as a few others watching Joyce roll a cigarette in the White Bull's smoking area didn't know what to think.

'Oh Jesus Christ, I'll spell it out to you bastards! There's a bunch of water here that the farmers own. Three tiers of it. And for the first time in our nation's history, we've had to import wheat! Fucking wheat! You wouldn't read about it, would you?'

Each reporter shook their head, except for the nice young lady from Prime just down the road.

'Well, you certainly don't read things on the television, do you?'

The Prime reporter shook her head.

Joyce erratically slapped his breast pockets.

'Fuck me, do any of you have a lighter?'

The former Deputy Prime Minister then lit his cigarette backwards before continuing his story about throwing rocks at the birdlife the last time he visited a full Lake Eyre back in 2010.

More to come.

The former Deputy Prime Minister then lit his cigarette backwards before continuing his story about throwing rocks at the birdlife the last time he visited a full Lake Eyre back in 2010.

OUR NECKLESS NOBLE SAVAGES

Censorship laws have all but failed the sewer of memes and pornography known as the internet, and our rising stars in the national rugby league are a case in point. The next generation of Immortals have a whole new range of social issues that aren't strictly linked to the traditional toxicities of footy club culture.

Today's NRL players are unable to have sex without sharing the experience with others. They are unable to do cocaine without filming themselves doing cocaine, and they can't stop betting on their own fucking matches.

While our women's sports stars are able to avoid scandal because most of them have to spend their off-field time holding 9–5 jobs to support their careers, the highly paid, under-occupied neckless titans of the rugby league are fast becoming a completely separate breed of public figure.

AFL and rugby union have always been known for their extremely effective rug-sweeping techniques, while the NRL seems to treat any fuck-ups as a form of unpaid marketing.

Many of the boys are now verging on 'influencer' status through social media, along with their long-suffering wives and girlfriends, some of whom are now running seminars on anti-vaxxing. The rise of these off-field profiles have instilled even more recklessness into the players – as many now realise they don't necessarily need the game to make a quid.

We all know how the saying goes: but in this world nothing can be said to be certain, except death, taxes and rugby league scandals . . . Except the 2018–19 rugby league off-season has completely raised the bar. Assaults, drug charges, sex tapes, betting scandals – from the players to the board members, it was absolutely schizophrenic.

Chairman of the code, Former Queensland Premier Peter Beattie, who was only 12 months into the role, had to pull the jigger on these wild stallions.

Together with CEO Todd Greenberg, Beattie developed the 'No-Fault Policy' which allows the NRL to stand a player down without prejudice if they are charged with a criminal offence which carries a maximum jail sentence of 11 years or more.

The new rule seemed to work. The boys pulled their heads in. Although some would argue that the commencement of round 1 may have had more to do with it. Rugby league players don't commit crimes when they are warming down in an ice bath.

Either way, things are all good for now. The Greatest Game Of All remains great.

NRL Integrity Unit Quietly Impressed Players Lasted 11 Days Before The First Scandal Of The Year

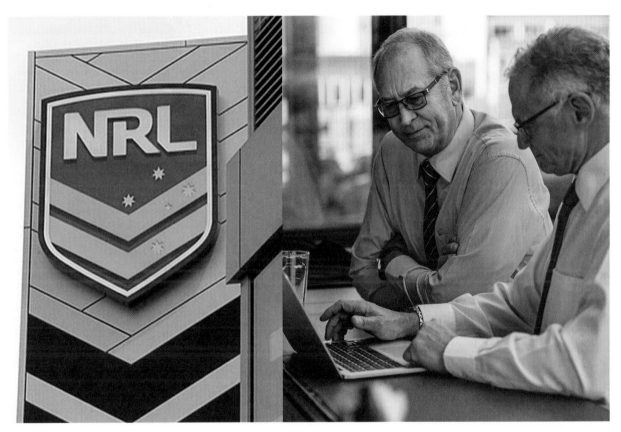

SOME TIME THIS AFTERNOON, a video emerged online showcasing one of the National Rugby League's brightest young prospects engaging in a sex act.

The Advocate's legal team have urged the sports reporters to err on the side of caution as this type of scandal can often lead to some city-based lawyer having to grease up their wrists and write a few cease and desists.

However, the video is available online and on the dark web as well.

Nevertheless, the NRL's Integrity Unit has told reporters a short time ago outside their headquarters in the nation's most unliveable city that they're quietly impressed that the players and their staff have lasted 11 days into this year without a scandal.

Bernie Greenpole, a senior investigator with the unit, spoke candidly to the media about the latest scandal shortly before 3 pm this afternoon.

'Not a bad effort,' he said. 'A few more days and we would've been in rugby union territory. Even then, it wouldn't be that bad. Just a Christian bloke telling folk on Instagram that he's off the gays in a big way.

'Instead, we have a bloke being filmed doing what a lot of young, virile Australians do whenever they have a dull minute among themselves. Soccer players often need less time than that! Anyway, we're investigating said video now and we'll let you know how it goes.'

More to come.

NRL CEO Calls For Every Player To Be Given Copy Of *Red Dead Redemption 2* In Effort To Keep Them Occupied

THE NRL HAS CALLED for drastic new measures to be implemented today, in an attempt to combat the extended run of off-field indiscretions.

Following a horror off-season where the game's players have repeatedly been unable to steer clear of trouble, NRL CEO Todd Greenberg has explained there will be some form of intervention.

The game's boss announced at a press conference this afternoon that every single player contracted to the NRL will be given a copy of *Red Dead Redemption 2*, and a console to play it on if required.

Greenberg explained that he hopes the extremely popular game can go some way towards stemming the tide of bad publicity.

'This whole debacle has gone too far,' Greenberg said today. 'These morons need something to keep them occupied, and when they've got a solid few months away from a regular season, you can see quite clearly how prone they are to acting up. If I'm honest, the best solution would be a 51-week season, but for obvious reasons we aren't allowed to do that, so we need to improvise.'

Greenberg explained that by coercing the players into wanting to spend their free time playing *Red Dead Redemption 2* he hopes to keep them out of trouble.

'If that doesn't work I'm quitting and just waiting until a job at the FFA or something opens up.'

NRL Edges Ahead Of The Nationals In Race For The Biggest Off-Season

THE GREATEST GAME ON EARTH has put its nose in front of the proverbial tractor fire that is the National Party today in the race to have the most counterproductive and controversial off-season.

While our public servants in Canberra have a much longer break than our rugby league–playing heroes, the Nationals held a commanding lead heading into the new year as many of their most senior members got up to no good.

Speaking to the media this morning from the deck of his Echuca riverboat, Nationals leader Michael McCormack flipped through yesterday's edition of *The Australian* as he fielded questions from journalists.

'Yes,' he said, wiping some errant scrambled eggs off his holiday beard. 'We plan to get back at the NRL in the coming weeks. We've already had a few stellar efforts. A real man-of-the-match performance by Andrew "The Side Doggy Country Boy" Broad, and I don't have to bring up the whole Barnaby soap opera.

'But this Napa episode has got us heading back to the drawing board.

Maybe we could get [Nigel] Scullion to recreate the second Napa video with Warren "Kingaroy Kingfish" Truss shadow-boxing? That's an idea. Warren has a great sense of humour.'

Our reporter reached out to the National Rugby League for comment but only received a short statement acknowledging that something had gone awry during the off-season and the Integrity Unit is now run off its feet.

More to come.

NRL Considers Implementing China-Style Social Credit System For Players After Off-Season From Hell

IN AN EFFORT TO QUELL poor player behaviour, the National Rugby League is toying with the idea of implementing a 'China-style' social credit system for players whereby certain privileges and benefits would be taken away as punishment for missteps and criminal offences.

Speaking to the media this morning in Sydney, our nation's worst place, NRL CEO Todd Greenberg explained that he's 'sick and tired' of having to deal with poor behaviour in the competition and he's 'looking at options' to remedy the problems God's game has in its culture.

'One of our ideas is to introduce a social credit system like they have in China,' he said. 'So for example, players like Cooper Cronk and the rent-a-Pom Burgess boys, they don't have anything to worry about. Well, maybe a bit, but comparatively not. But for players like Mitchell Pearce, Dylan Napa and all the other off-season ████████, certain privileges would be taken away. Like travelling by air. Say, for example, they'd have to get the train to Brisbane or Melbourne for an away game. Go on a P&O across the Tasman to play the Warriors. You know, things like that.'

The system would be updated in real time, with players having an app installed on their phone that tracks who and what they message – as well as their position at all times.

However, a representative from the Rugby League Players Association has lashed out at 'Chrome dome Todd', saying that it's unfair to target

just the players in this – that coaching and support staff as well as NRL executives should also be part of this proposed system.

'Do they think we are stupid?' said the official. 'If the walls of every bathhouse around the country could talk, they'd tell you it's not just the league players who love a bit of a rub down. It's top to bottom – the whole culture of this sport is rotten. All we're saying here at the Rugby League Players Association is that he who is without sin, cast the first stone.'

The first stone was reportedly cast by Cooper Cronk a short time later, who threw a rock through the rear windscreen of Greenberg's Citroën C4 Cactus.

More to come.

> *Speaking to the media this morning in Sydney, our nation's worst place, NRL CEO Todd Greenberg explained that he's 'sick and tired' of having to deal with poor behaviour in the competition and he's 'looking at options' to remedy the problems God's game has in its culture.*

New 3D Map Shows Sharp Increase In NRL Players' iPhones At Bottom Of Sydney Harbour

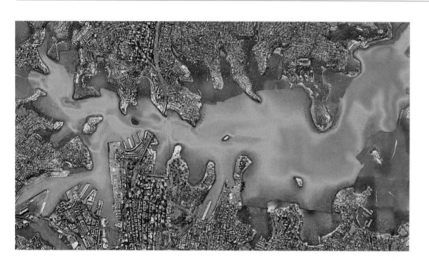

'The NRL just wanted to make sure all the players had done as they were told and thrown their fucken phones away,' said Professor Fulton. This follows the social media firestorm last month that saw footage emerge showing a number of players and their dodgy hanger-on mates performing sex acts and doing heaps of cocaine.

A FREELANCE TEAM of underwater geo-mapping experts have today revealed some of the spectacular 3D images of the Sydney Harbour floor and its surprising contents.

Some of the findings show very interesting changes since last year's surveyor maps, the most surprising being the thousands of abandoned iPhones belonging to nervous NRL players next to every bridge and waterside highway in the city.

Four hydrographic surveyors at Sydney Ports keep an ever-vigilant eye on the bottom of the harbour to make sure possible dangers in the depths do not disrupt water traffic around Port Jackson.

'There must be an iPhone for every footballer in the city in there,' said lead researcher, Professor Dallas Fulton. 'Luckily none of the phones is still working, which I think was the point.'

With funding from the NRL the scientists used a 'multibeam echo sounder' system, valued at $750,000, to make detailed 3D maps of the harbour floor.

'The NRL just wanted to make sure all the players had done as they were told and thrown their fucken phones away,' said Professor Fulton.

This follows the social media firestorm last month that saw footage emerge showing a number of players and their dodgy hanger-on mates performing sex acts and doing heaps of cocaine.

Australia's finance sector and the Federal Government say that they are relieved this kind of media shitstorm has coincided with the very concerning findings released as part of the Banking Royal Commission.

Similar 3D maps are currently underway in the major water systems of Newcastle, Brisbane and Townsville.

No one cares about Titans players.

More to come.

Adidas Develop New NRL-Style Footy Boot Featuring Ankle Bracelet Compatibility

MOVING WITH THE TIMES, popular sports brand Adidas have today announced the release of a new range of football boots.

The second largest sportswear company in the world made the announcement this morning, unveiling their new styles ahead of the 2019 winter season.

Notably, the new range will feature a new cutting-edge 'NRL boot', which will combine the added ankle support popular with modern-day players with the added ability to attach an electronic monitoring bracelet if required.

The new feature comes after the shitshow that was the 2018–19 NRL off-season, which saw many of the game's players land themselves in hot water.

The head of Adidas in Australia told *The Advocate* that they are expecting the new style to be a big hit.

'Our NRL boot is the perfect bit of kit for the elite and semi-professional rugby league player on the eastern seaboard,' he explained. 'The flexibility the boot offers puts our rivals to shame, really. It allows the authorities to monitor your behaviour if you have favourable bail conditions given to you because you're an NRL player, or if you are given a non-custodial sentence. And if you just want to get used to the feel of it, just in case you do something crook during an end-of-season trip away down the track, then it's the perfect boot for you.'

The boot is expected to be on shelves across the country by the end of the week.

R Kelly And Chris Brown Announced As Pre-Match Entertainment For 2019 NRL Grand Final

IN A DESPERATE BID to resurrect their once wholesome and family-friendly image, the NRL have today decided to spend big dollars on flying out some of the biggest recording artists in music history for the 2019 NRL Grand Final.

This comes after an absolutely chaotic off-season that has resulted in roughly 66 different reported off-field scandals.

The NRL's Integrity Unit has reportedly tripled in size since the Grand Final's final buzzer on 30 September 2018, as the code desperately recruits waves of new administration staff to sift through the piles of new incident reports.

From drugs to abusive behaviour to sex tapes to exotic animal trafficking to bashing Uber drivers, the playing ranks of the NRL have been busy over the last few months doing a little extra marketing that no one asked for.

However, the game's ruling body is hoping that today's huge announcement will go some way towards stemming the bleeding this week.

'This is a pretty big coup for us,' explained Saul Good, the head of the NRL's Culture Department and the driving force behind booking American R'n'B artists R Kelly and Chris Brown for the 2019 Grand Final entertainment.

'These two artists align perfectly with our brand and the thing our game stands for. Which is love, respect and good times.

'Like us, and our players, these artists have managed to brush aside and ignore damning allegations in an attempt to block out the noise and carry on as normal, so they'll be up for the occasion. And I'm sure they'll take the heat off our players. And all that aside, I'm sure they'll put on a hell of a show. It's the best way to turn on the ignition to our biggest night of the year [haha].'

There have also been talks between the NRL and the Sydney Theatre Company to secure Geoffrey Rush as the guest performer of the Australian national anthem.

More to come.

Weirdo NRL Player Prefers To Make Love Without Any Mates In The Room

Rockstar Games Announces The Release Of Long-Awaited *GTA: NRL Off-Season*

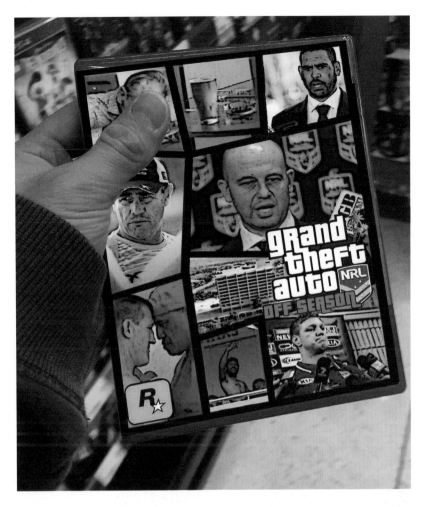

THE PROVERBIAL BIN FIRE of a 2019 off-season for The Greatest Game of All appears to have attracted the attention of a prominent New York–based video game publisher, Rockstar Games.

Following the record-breaking releases of *Red Dead Redemption 2* on all consoles and *Grand Theft Auto V* on PC, the gamer rumour mill has been flat chat for months with theories about what Rockstar would turn their craft to next.

Today, it has all been confirmed. A video game based around rugby league, and not necessarily the game.

GTA: NRL Off-Season will follow the careers of three separate characters and explore the highs, lows and unbridled chaos that comes with professional rugby league football.

The first character to be introduced is Arthur Payne OAM, a senior club executive from an affluent beachside NRL club still reeling from a high-profile affair with an Insta-model cheerleader thirty years his junior. Arthur is swaying closer to the crosshairs of both the club board members and ICAC, after a would-be whistleblower discovers that he had prior knowledge of a team doctor administering performance-enhancing drugs to his players. As a former Kings Cross police officer, Arthur calls on his old connections from his days as a copper – both in and outside of the police force – for some favours.

The second character is 20-year-old South Brisbane Dally M prediction, Lolesio Prince. A promising junior from Logan Brothers who has just returned from his year of Mormon missionary work in Tonga, Lolesio is put between a rock and a hard place after an innocent night out at Sizzler with a group of bikie-affiliated childhood friends results in a shootout in the car park of the Hyperdome. With a man dead, Lolesio must find a way to pay the bikies to protect his identity and help distance himself from the ongoing investigations, while also providing for his two young daughters and bringing glory back to the Maroon jersey.

The third and most prominent story arc follows Kyle Coorey, a colourful racing identity and bumbling player-manager from a prominent Lebanese-Australian construction dynasty in Western Sydney. After his cash cow snaps an achilles during an alcohol-fuelled pub fight at the Plantation Hotel in Coffs Harbour, and his most recent recruit is coward-punched outside Mooseheads in Canberra, Kyle recognises a pattern. A racing debt from yesteryear threatens the lives and on-field form of his entire stable of players. After discovering links to the NSW Labor Party, Kyle realises the rabbit hole runs a lot deeper than Rosehill.

GTA: NRL Off-Season is expected to be released around November this year, when the NRL off-season starts and sports journalists are looking for shit to write about.

NRL To Enforce Mandatory Nokia 3310 Policy For All Players

ALL NRL PLAYERS will be forced to hand over any smartphones, tablets or GoPros that they may own, in a recent policy announced today and backed by all clubs.

While the Queensland NRL clubs appear to be living up to their reputation as polite, community-minded footballing institutions made up of gentlemen, the recent riffraff from down south have forced the hand of the game's CEO today.

This follows the news that NSW police today charged Penrith Panthers third-string star Tyrone May after he allegedly featured in two sex tapes that were leaked last week. The 22-year-old utility has been charged with two counts of recording intimate images without consent, and two counts of disseminating images without consent.

Speaking to the media today at a press conference somewhere in that shithole harbour city, NRL CEO Todd Greenberg says that as of today, all players must hand over any communication devices made after 1 September 2000.

'This is a hard-line approach. There's no WhatsApp groups in these bad boys,' he said, while showing off the iconic Nokia 3310 – which is remembered as one of the most successful phones of its era, with 126 million units sold worldwide.

'We've ordered in thousands of them, there aren't even cameras on these things. Just SMS features and really expensive phone calls.'

Greenberg believes that by removing smartphones from the equation, rugby league players will be able to learn how to woo women the old-fashioned way – as opposed to organising porn shoots through Instagram DMs.

'They need to learn the hard way like my generation did,' he says. 'Texting chicks on a numbered keypad teaches a man a lot about patience and respect.

'. . . And when both parties are finally comfortable enough with each other to partake in a full-on orgy with their teammates – there's no way these dumb cunts will be able to film it and share it with the world.'

NRL Shouts Players Free Piss And Topless Waitresses To Celebrate Two Weeks Without A Scandal

'CONSIDER OUR EPIDEMIC of off-field incidents resolved,' shouted NRL CEO Todd Greenberg as he loosened his tie and gave a fist-pump to the roaring crowd of players and sponsors.

'We did it. The boys are playing great footy on the field and are quiet as church mice off the field!'

These were the comments heard shouted through a PA system at last night's celebratory Mad Monday in March event hosted at the NRL headquarters, celebrating two full weeks without a scandal in the rugby league.

While it is not yet known what the direct cause of this lull in assaults, sex tapes and alcohol-fuelled incidents is, the NRL and the Nine Network have been quick to treat themselves.

With a hand-your-phone-over-at-the-door policy, topless waitresses and a never-ending open bar, executives and players tied one on last night to celebrate the 14 days since a headline.

Greenberg, who has been under siege from the media over the last few months, appeared to be the most elated at this new milestone.

'People were asking me to stand players down forever,' he roared. 'People were asking me and Peter to stand down. But you know what? I'm not fucken leaving! We're not fucken leaving! The show goes on!!!'

Greenberg then broke out into a *Wolf of Wall Street*–style chest thump as the hundreds of contract NRL players in the room began to hum along.

'Uh-hummm!' echoed out through surrounding parklands. 'Uh hummmm!'

While media analysts say this current hot streak of little-to-no NRL scandals could be related entirely to the fact that there is much scarier shit happening in the news, as well as a NSW state election happening this week and a federal election in the next few months, the players say it's all because they simply decided to pull their heads in.

'It also helps that we are now either training or playing for 85 per cent of the week,' said one heavily tattooed NRL recruit, who chose to remain anonymous because he's married and probably shouldn't be behaving like that.

'We'll see how we go. It's always a long winter.'

While it is not yet known what the direct cause of this lull in assaults, sex tapes and alcohol-fuelled incidents is, the NRL and the Nine Network have been quick to treat themselves.

One Nation Consults NRL For Tips On How To Deal With Leaked Videos You'd Prefer People Don't See

PAULINE HANSON has today paid an unexpected visit to the NRL Central to seek advice from the rugby league executives on how to best deal with damaging video footage that has the potential to fuck your entire organisation.

This follows the release of a damning two-part investigation into One Nation's attempts to undermine Australian democracy by meeting with American gun lobbyists and asking for $20 million in exchange for weakening our nation's firearm laws.

Pauline Hanson and two of her incredibly lightweight political staffers were caught on hidden cameras by Al Jazeera journalists claiming that the Port Arthur massacre was a government conspiracy, while also discussing plans to solicit legally grey campaign funds from controversial foreign gun lobbyists.

After already trying twice to defuse the humiliating documentary, Hanson briefly spoke to CEO Todd Greenberg before discovering he was Jewish, and therefore an enemy of her political party.

She then opted to swallow her pride and meet with former Queensland Labor Premier and current NRL Chairman Peter Beattie, who she considered the lesser of two evils.

Peter Beattie allegedly told Pauline Hanson her best bet was to introduce a no-fault ruling that would see the immediate dismissal of any employees who are facing up to 11 years in prison.

Pauline Hanson is believed to have said this might be a bit difficult considering the gun-loving white supremacists she has been vetting for pre-selection for the upcoming federal election.

Beattie then told the One Nation leader that realistically she's got no leg to stand on.

'Really, though, Pauline,' said Beattie. 'This is a bit more than just a sex tape. You are all caught on camera admitting to collusion with some of the most dangerous movements in world politics. It's a bit different when the footage shows you fucking a whole country without a kiss.'

NRL Players Advised To Win An Oscar If They Want To Survive #█████ Allegations

THE MOUTH-BREATHING WORKING-CLASS MORONS who play that neckless brand of 'sportsball' for a living have been advised today that if they want to behave however they want, they should █████ █████ the arts.

█████████████████████████
█████████████████████████
substantial win █████████████
█████████████ Sydney newspaper
█████████████████████████
█████████████████ the █████
█████████████████████████
█████████ towards █████████
█████████████████████████
█████████████████████████
performance of █████████████
█████████████████████████
█████████████████████████

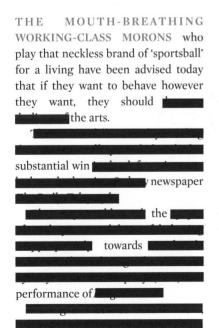

██████████ testimony █████████
██████████ testified █████████
█████████████████████████
immediate suspension in the NRL, █████████████████████████
█████████ because tattooed men who say the word 'youse' are much more likely to have █████████████
█████████████████████████
█████████████████████████
█████████████████████ found in █████ favour and said █████████
█████████████████████ truth █████████████████ inner city leftie boomers █████████████████████
█████████████████████████
than the █████████████████████
█████████████████████

NRL players across all clubs have

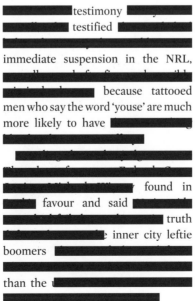

██████████████████████████
██████████████████████████
become a hot topic of conversation in the terrace house dining rooms of Balmain and South Yarra.

██████████████████████████
██████████ said an █████████ rugby league player █████████████
██████ and fined █████████████
██████████████████████████
██████████████████████████

'O█████████████████████████
██████████████████████████
██████████████████████████
██████████████████████████
█████████. And they are making me pose for the Archibalds.'

PELL IN
A CELL

At the time of writing, Australia's most senior Catholic is appealing his child sex convictions, so in the interest of preventing this book from being pulped via a court order, we must tread carefully.

When Cardinal Pell was first convicted of these disgusting, despicable crimes against children, the case broke on a handful of news websites before it was removed without a trace. People were confused. Rumours were born out of the blackout but nobody was allowed to say the name.

A few months later, however, the waters of justice had reached the top of the dam wall and began to trickle down the spillway.

Then all of a sudden, the gates were lifted and the news flooded out into the populace.

Cardinal Pell was guilty.

The news was covered by every major media outlet in the world. Cardinal Pell is the most senior member of the Vatican to be convicted of child sexual abuse.

However, the Vatican's Treasurer refused to return to Victoria to face his accusations, despite being effectively ex-communicated by the Pope...

That was until a very catchy song was penned by the spooky man of the west, Tim Minchin. It eventually became unavoidable. Pell finally came home.

For now, Cardinal Pell sits in a prison cell he will likely spend the rest of his life in.

And now the Catholic Church can move on and continue to be a shining beacon of light by which everybody should live. Everything has gone back to normal.

Or the nation could start taxing them, which is an idea.

Local Priest Mistakes Man's Confession About Sex Crimes For A Job Application

CONTROVERSIAL LOCAL CATHOLIC PRIEST Father Ricepell has today embarrassed both himself and an anonymous penitent – who had approached the confession booth to seek penance for historical sex crimes.

Father Ricepell, who was recently moved to the Diamantina area after running into 'a mischief' in Tamworth several years ago, was left confused by the man's admission that he had actively crossed the line of sexual consent in several circumstances over the last few decades.

In Catholic teaching, the Sacrament of Penance is the method of the church by which individual men and women may confess sins committed after baptism and have them absolved by God through the administration of a priest.

'I should have just forgiven him.

That's what he was there for,' said Father Ricepell. 'Instead, I offered him a job! He really wasn't expecting that.'

With the highest-ranking Catholic in Australia currently facing charges in Victoria for child sex crimes, and the Royal Commission's findings that over 20 per cent of clergymen over the last century have been involved in child abuse crimes, Father Ricepell says it's easy to mistake paedophiles for aspiring priests.

'He wasn't interested. Even when I mentioned the job perks. I told him all he needs to do is begin drinking heavily and actively speak out against gay marriage – and then maybe we can find him some work. He seems to have everything else sorted. An undying sense of guilt and a lust for the vulnerable.'

The Royal Commission into Institutional Responses to Child Abuse has found that more than 20 per cent of the members of some Catholic institutions were allegedly involved in child sexual abuse.

A report has found nearly 2,000 Catholic Church figures, including priests, religious brothers, sisters and employees, were identified as alleged perpetrators.

The fact that this number constitutes 'a little bit more than a few' means that the church must now refer to the minority of clergymen that have a habit of molesting children as 'roughly 20 per cent'.

'Anyway. He left here in a bit of a huff. I told him to give me a call when he's ready to wear the cloth.'

Pell To Be Exposed To Months Of Humiliating Media Focusing On His Sex Life

THE FRIENDS AND ALLIES of Australia's highest-ranking Catholic say they are worried the media storms surrounding the hearing about the historical sex offence charges against him will expose the community to months of demeaning rhetoric focused on his personal life.

This comes now that the hearing is open to the public following several days of closed court evidence from his accusers.

Pell returns to Melbourne Magistrates' Court today for a committal hearing that will determine whether he will stand trial over charges involving multiple complainants.

'We are really worried that this is going to open up a fierce public debate over the personal life of both Cardinal Pell and his friends,' says the Archbishop of Betoota South Diocese, Father Rog Spighter.

'This does not need to be settled in a public forum. We believe people will be donating large sums of money to advertisers in an attempt to victimise Cardinal Pell.'

The pre-trial hearing began on 5 March but was closed to the public as the complainants gave evidence, as required by law in sex offence cases. The hearing opened to the public on Wednesday afternoon, with volunteer researcher and retired academic Bernard Barrett giving evidence about his work with victim advocacy group Broken Rites.

Defence barrister Robert Richter QC accused Mr Barrett of making up allegations and trying to 'pin' historical sex offences on Pell in a campaign against the Catholic community.

'You make up representations on the website and elsewhere accusing the church of covering up sexual abuse, is that right? This cannot be good for the mental health of Catholics who just want to raise families and live a normal life like the rest of us.'

Abbott Doubles Down On Conservative Vote And Says He'll Knight George Pell If He Wins Power Again

TONY ABBOTT HAS REVEALED controversial plans to offer a knighthood to embattled cardinal George Pell should he win power again over Malcolm Turnbull.

Speaking to the House this afternoon, the former Prime Minister said he's looking to 'out-conservative the conservatives in his party' in a move aimed at stealing right-faction favour away from incumbent leader Peter Dutton.

'If this doesn't work then I guess there's no pleasing them,' said Abbott. 'People have told me that if I knight Cardinal Pell, it'll make me even more unpopular – which I find hard to believe. The hardest thing, in my opinion, will be passing the necessary legislation through both houses that'll bring knighthood back. I don't give a fuck. This is my Everest and I'll climb it.'

The Advocate reached out to the Catholic Church for comment on the proposed plan to knight Jesus' representative in Australia but only received a Holy Bible laced with a white powder in return.

Nevertheless, a number of replies were received from other members of the House.

The Member for Kennedy, the Hon. Bob Katter, took time out of his busy afternoon to fax his handwritten response back to our offices.

'Gentleman, I received your email and yes, I am concerned,' wrote Mr Katter. 'There were many parts of Tony's speech to parliament this afternoon that didn't sit well with me. Knighting Cardinal Pell, in my opinion, would be a grave mistake to make. At times, the speech made me physically ill. It was nothing short of disgusting. However, I couldn't look away. Now, let me talk to you about this new vanadium business in Charters Towers ...'

The 44-page response from Mr Katter is still being printed by the fax machine and it will be published in full once it's finished and our intern figures out how to get the scanner working again.

More to come.

Catholic Church's Views On Homosexuality Prevent Pell From Using The Spacey Defence

THE HISTORIC SEXUAL ABUSE ALLEGATIONS levelled against Australia's highest-ranking clergyman have been further complicated by the fact that crying gay is not an option for Cardinal Pell, if he wants the Catholic Church to keep paying for his lawyers.

This comes as the 76-year-old begins to get desperate in his attempts at evading criminal prosecution for ruining the lives of several young children who were in his duty of care over the last century.

The Catholic Church has made it clear that the Spacey Defence is not an option.

According to the American Law Society, the Spacey Defence is defined as: *Publicly proclaiming that you're gay when you get called out for committing a horrific crime.*

It comes from when Hollywood actor Kevin Spacey was accused by former child star Anthony Rapp of trying to molest him when he was 14, and Kevin Spacey responded by saying he's gay.

However, this legal loophole isn't an option for Cardinal Pell, as the Catholic Church has made it clear that they are much more inclined to defend someone facing multiple allegations of paedophilia then someone who is openly gay.

The 76-year-old faced a directions hearing in the County Court in Melbourne after being committed to stand trial on multiple charges on Tuesday.

The court heard Cardinal Pell's defence lawyers and prosecutors agreed he should face two trials, due to the fact that he is charged over separate sets of allegations 20 years apart.

It is likely that the first trial will deal with allegations that he committed sexual offences at Melbourne's St Patrick's Cathedral in the 1990s when he was Archbishop of Melbourne.

If the trials are split, a second jury would then hear allegations relating to swimming pools in the regional Victorian city of Ballarat in the 1970s when he was a young priest.

The court heard each trial is likely to run for about five weeks.

Canberra To Host Nation's First Pell-Testing Trial To Help Churchgoers Identify Dodgy Priests

WITH MANY CHURCH SERVICES to come in 2019, including the very popular Easter Mass, the perennial debate over Pell-testing in Australia has once again kicked on with health professionals, politicians and commentators weighing in.

Australia's first Pell-testing trial, held at Canberra's annual Catholic Fair this year, has seen plenty of critics come out of the woodwork saying testing only results in more atheists.

But there is no solid evidence to show that Pell-testing leads to churchgoers choosing the life of a non-believer and going to hell. In fact, there are multiple studies and trials indicating that Pell-testing often results in fewer people going to hell.

By simply checking a suspicious priest's heart rate and asking him to name his favourite Australian artists, experts say they can almost immediately identify a rock spider with potential to cause harm.

The ACT government's announcement to allow Pell-testing tents at all church fairs follows the lifting of a nationwide suppression order, allowing media to report that George Pell has been found guilty of sexually abusing two choirboys when he was Archbishop of Melbourne.

While conservative commentators have been quick to defend Cardinal Pell against the convictions handed to him by a jury of his peers and years of police investigation, Canberra has decided a preventative approach may be the best route to avoid any more lives being ruined.

Other initiatives to help break down the rampant culture of child sex crimes in the Catholic Church have also been put forward, with some experts suggesting that maybe if we allow Catholic priests to get married and live a normal life, we might not end up with so many creeps deciding to join the clergy.

Other radical suggestions like taxing the church or not forcing religion onto people below the age of consent have been immediately shunned by the devout rock choppers in both the ALP and Liberal Party.

See Ya Later, Cunt

The entire planet is now free to tell Cardinal George Pell to get fucked today, after finally being able to talk openly about the stuff that we were all talking about months ago.

Pope Francis Spends Morning Dodging Phone Calls From An 'Irate' Jesus Christ Demanding Answers

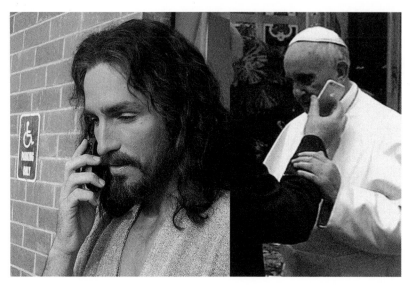

THE HEAD OF THE CATHOLIC CHURCH has reportedly spent the early-morning hours in Rome dodging phone calls from Jesus H. Christ, the man he represents here on this hellish, godforsaken rock floating through space.

Pope Francis, a mildly unpopular 82-year-old Sagittarian, has been handed the papal iPhone a number of times by his concerned aides – only for him to push their arm away in panic.

'I can't speak to him right now,' said the Pope.

'Sorry, Him. What am I supposed to say? Sorry for hiring the bloke? It's 2 am here and I'm not in the mood for a tongue-lashing. Just tell Him that I'm asleep. If he tells you to wake me up, say I've taken some Ambien and can't be roused.'

The Advocate reached out to God via the Betoota Heights Hillsong Church but have yet to receive a reply.

However, the overly polite and creepy Hillsong pastor said we'd get one if we signed up to come one Friday night and clap our hands and shake our can to the gospel.

Our reporter also spoke briefly to the Catholic Archbishop of Betoota, who refused to acknowledge the existence of Cardinal Pell and threatened *The Advocate* with defamation.

Nevertheless Jesus did respond to our reporter's request for comment from the Holy Spirit.

Speaking to *The Advocate* candidly via a writhing tongue-speaking priest, Mr Christ said that he's 'livid' with his representatives on Earth and he 'wants some God-damn answers'.

'What in blue Christ is going on down there!' murmured the seizing priest. 'Don't make me come down there, I'll bin the lot of you! And can you tell that fucking Pope to stop screening my calls? I've tried his landline, Facebook, Instagram and mobile. I want some fucking answers!'

The priest then stopped his violent writhing and regained consciousness.

More to come.

'Just tell Him that I'm asleep. If he tells you to wake me up, say I've taken some Ambien and can't be roused.'

'I Don't Think There Is Enough Evidence To Convict Pell,' Says Man Who Invaded Iraq On A Hunch

THE MAN RESPONSIBLE for thousands of deaths in a hostile invasion of the Middle East off the back of rumours he had heard about Saddam Hussein harbouring weapons of mass destruction, has today said he's not so sure that we should be rushing to condemn George Pell.

The December conviction of Cardinal Pell, and today's subsequent pre-sentencing hearing, has come as a shock to many Howard-era Liberal Party figures, who are remembered for their colossal campaign strategy that saw the Coalition sway many conservative voters away from the traditionally Catholic ALP in the mid-90s.

Former Prime Minister John Howard appears to be the most shocked of them all, even going as far as offering a character reference for the cardinal, written after he was made aware that Pell has been found guilty of sexually abusing two choirboys when he was Archbishop of Melbourne.

Pell's barrister has tendered to the judge the statements of ten character witnesses including friends and former staff. All were aware that he has been convicted.

'Those people love him ... None of them believe he is capable of this,' said his barrister.

This also comes after Pell has been sacked from his role as the Vatican treasurer, the third-highest-ranking figure in the Holy City.

Former Prime Minister John Howard, however, just isn't sure.

'I'll have to speak with George and Tony ... but I'm pretty suspicious about these claims,' he said.

'I'm not big on rushing into things like this, especially when it all looks like a bit of hearsay. And when a lot of people could get hurt. I feel like some people might have an ulterior agenda here, and I don't think we should play into their hands without some solid evidence.'

Katter Not Going Near It

DESPITE RELENTLESS REQUESTS from the Australian media to give a fucked-up quote about what is going on down in Melbourne at the moment, Bob Katter MP has remained strong in his efforts to swerve you-know-what.

The maverick North Queensland MP has been very careful to not give a quote about anything, because, you know, they had a very similar thing happening up in the Isa back in the day – and it's not something he wants to go near.

In fact, if he had his way, this whole thing would be sorted out behind the courthouse with a length of hose and some nylon fishing line.

When asked for comment yesterday afternoon, Katter told reporters there was only one thing on his mind, and that is how on earth they are gonna rebuild the cattle industry in flood-ravaged north-west Queensland – after the Nightwatchman spent an entire fortnight being put over the barrel at

the hands of the intimidating silver vixen who replaced Turnbull.

He also spent 45 minutes once again addressing the very blatant bias shown towards southern Queensland footballers in the Maroons selections.

At time of press, our reporters were being treated to Katter's 19-minute rendition of an old Irish ballad about shooting the Black and Tans.

If he had his way, this whole thing would be sorted out behind the courthouse with a length of hose and some nylon fishing line.

Cardinal Pell's Moral High Horse Set Free To Live Among The Wild Brumbies Of The Snowy River

AS THE LOW DOG who redefined Catholic guilt, George Pell, spends his first days in prison, it was revealed that his high horse has retired to live as a wild brumby in the Snowy Mountains.

Pell and his high horse were previously known as the successful duo that used ancient belief systems to prevent societal change on issues such as stem cell research, climate change and marriage equality.

While still wearing a racing bib with the VOTE NO logo emblazoned across it, the horse is now free to live life in the wild – without having to be trotted out as some sort of political authority every time a progressive issue is raised in public debate.

A representative of George Pell, who may or may not be a previous PM of Australia, stated that releasing the cardinal's high horse into the Snowies is the most humane course of action, now that gay marriage has passed and the cardinal is a convicted pedo.

'This horse will play a part in damaging an integral Australian ecosystem in the name of saving face and promoting the idea that doing fuck-all about the environment is a good thing,' stated the spokesperson through wet eyes. 'I can't imagine a better send-off for this majestic animal. It's what Pell would want.

'Hopefully it doesn't get bitten by any poisonous snakes or insects, but I suppose it's done well over the last 77 years to have remained safe around such a prolific rock spider.'

Abbott Asks Hanson If She Has Any Neo-Nazi Contacts That Might Be Able To Protect Pell Inside

AFTER BEING DEVASTATED by the news that one of his favourite Catholic figures is now facing the repercussions of raping children, former Prime Minister Tony Abbott is doing everything he can to ensure Cardinal Pell remains safe over the next three to six years.

As Australia's best-known Catholic politician, Tony Abbott has long defended his long-standing friend, Cardinal George Pell – even after he was convicted of child sex crimes in December, and subsequently sentenced today.

The news has shocked the world, with the once third-highest-ranking figure in the Catholic Church likely to spend the rest of his life in prison, where he will join the thousands of incarcerated felons whose lives were destroyed in childhood by institutionalised abuse orchestrated by figures like Pell.

It is for this reason that Pell, who is facing six years in prison, is believed to be at extreme risk in the prison yard.

The Member for Warringah – whose irrationally devout brand of fundamental Catholicism is effectively the reason he was ousted from the country's top job and will likely be ousted from his blue ribbon Liberal electorate at the upcoming election – has today moved very quickly to provide a soft landing pad for Cardinal Pell when he arrives at Port Phillip this afternoon.

After giving up on his attempts at having a coherent conversation with

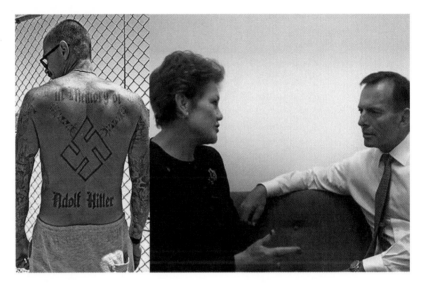

Independent neo-Nazi Senator Fraser Anning, Abbott continued down the hallways of parliament until he found Pauline.

'Pauline, love,' he said.

'Yes, dar . . . You're talking to me again are you?' responded Pauline.

'Haha, um, ahh, yes. Yes that would be the case,' said Abbott.

'How can I help ya?' she said.

Abbott then tried his luck at politely maintaining a respectful level of eye contact with the female subordinate.

'It's just that, um, ahh, I'm a bit nervous that my mate George is going to get the old Breville toaster in the pillowcase tonight. Was just wondering if you had any contacts in the white supremacist underworld that might be able to protect him … For a handsome fee, of course. The Catholics pay top dollar for protection.'

Pauline Hanson said she was honoured to be asked to help, and that she was pretty sure that Dane Sweetman was still getting around the Victorian prison system.

'Let me make a few calls, love. I can't promise you anything. These people don't really take kindly to rock spiders,' said Pauline. 'That's what I learnt while I was inside anyw–

'Actually . . .'

Pauline Hanson's eyes began to narrow as she started to remember the 14 months she spent in a Queensland women's prison after she was victimised by a smear campaign orchestrated by a young Howard minister named Tony Abbott.

'Actually, you can go and fuck yourself, Tony. How's that sound?'

'What NRL Team Does George Pell Play For?' Asks Wife Who's Been A Bit Distracted By MAFS

AFTER FINALLY BREAKING FREE from her trash TV–induced catatonic state late last night, local woman Angela Mason (34) has rushed to catch up with the Australian news cycle.

After weeks of dedicating every waking hour to the trials and tribulations of the young men and women who make up the bottom of the barrel in terms of Australian reality television, Angela is taking this opportunity to get up to date with what everyone else is talking about.

After opening up several news apps on her phone, the local primary school teacher was bombarded with thousands of backed-up news stories about the many different scandals and convictions that have filtered through the newsrooms this week.

'Oh wow. The NRL is really having a shocker,' she tells her husband, Joe. 'Like, this is really bad. These guys sound about as dumb as the blokes I've been watching on *Married At First Sight*.'

However, while deep in her news binge, it appears that Angela has made the mistake of mixing up two of the nation's most scandal-riddled institutions: the Catholic Church and the NRL.

As an atheist who doesn't like watching contact sport, it's understandable that Angela would confuse the highest-ranking figure in the Australian Catholic Church with a millennial footballer – given how fucked both those two organisations currently are.

The NRL off-season from hell, as it has been described, has involved just about every felony under the sun – except for the crimes Angela is currently associating it with.

'What NRL team does George Pell play for?' she asks her husband.

Joe, who can't be bothered explaining that while the NRL players are fucking bad, they aren't *that bad* – decides to see how long he can keep this going.

'Parra,' he says. 'Absolutely disgusting what he did.'

It's understandable that Angela would confuse the highest-ranking figure in the Australian Catholic Church with a millennial footballer – given how fucked both those two organisations currently are.

George Pell Starting To Worry After Abbott Fails To Answer Office Phone For Three Whole Days

THE NEWS OF ZALI STEGGALL'S comprehensive victory in Warringah has reportedly not yet made its way to the exercise yard of the Melbourne Assessment Prison.

This news comes as panic sets in for the recently incarcerated rock spider, Cardinal Pell, who feels he might be getting the silent treatment from his confidant and former Prime Minister Tony Abbott.

'He hasn't answered his office phone for days now,' says a distressed Pell, while waiting his turn to make yet another unanswered phone call in The Map. 'Was it something I said?'

Unfortunately for the former third-highest-ranking Catholic figure in the world, that phone number will never be answered again.

Independent MP Zali Steggall swept to victory in Saturday's federal election, taking 58 per cent of the two-party-preferred vote, with Abbott suffering a swing against him of almost 20 per cent.

Pell, who received a glowing character reference from the former Member for Warringah in the days after he was charged and convicted for historical child sex crimes, says he's starting to worry something bad might've happened.

'He usually answers the moment I ring,' says Pell. 'I would try his mobile, but he made me delete his number during the Royal Commission.'

The former Archbishop of both Sydney and Melbourne says being ghosted by Tony Abbott is the last thing he needs, on top of being the lowest of low in a prison populated by violent offenders.

'I've got no one else to talk to. He was the only one that answered my calls. He understood what it was like to be the victim of a politically motivated smear campaign.'

NIGHT OF
THE LONG
KNIVES

THE 2018 LIB SPILL

On 14 September 2015, armed with a pair of folded thick-framed reading glasses, Malcolm Turnbull ascended from his maligned role as Communications Minister to leader of the Liberal Government.

Considering this was the sixth leadership spill of the decade, former Prime Minister Tony Abbott should have been able to leave the role with his pride intact – as it is not too rare to be ousted by your own party anymore. However, the way Turnbull did it was particularly cruel.

It happened on the most important day in Abbott's professional career. The 40-year reunion for his elite North Shore private boarding school. Which was being hosted by him, on the lawns of Kirribilli House.

With the new added convenience of social media, Tony Abbott was humiliated in front of his true electorate. The only people he'd ever cared about impressing. The Old Boys. On his lawn. With their phones pinging in their pockets.

He didn't even have a chance to say goodbye to the old rowing mates. He was straight in a car to Canberra. But it was already over. Turnbull was so certain of his numbers that he showed very little humility when he took a blowtorch to the 28th Australian Prime Minister.

To this day, no one knows why Turnbull did it the way he did it. Was it because of the hospital passes that had been flicked to him by Abbott keeping him from taking the top job? Slashing the ABC budget and rolling out a sub-par copper wire NBN doesn't look good on a resume.

Was it because of the relentless humiliation he had suffered at the hands of Abbott's confidante Peta Credlin? Was it simply the age-old competitiveness of Sydney's New Money versus Sydney's Old Money?

Whatever it was, it wasn't put to bed that day.

Abbott hung around for three years throwing peanuts from the back bench. Every political firefight Turnbull faced was doused with accelerants by Abbott. The plebiscite, the citizenship scandals, the bleaching reef and the plastic bag ban.

As time wore on, Abbott's allies of undervalued old drunkards grew. He was soon joined by Barnaby on the back bench, and it became very clear that he had a guy on the inside of the cabinet. It was time to orchestrate revenge.

We don't know who pulled the trigger and what their end game was, but we do know that Peter Dutton flew his family down to Canberra to hear daddy's victory speech. Once again, Turnbull showed us a little of that Goldman Sachs psychopath that he'd tried so hard to hide with the brown leather jacket.

And once again, the Liberal Party's ultra conservative heavyweights were tricked by the Pied Piper from Point Piper. The numbers were stacked and the far-right villains came out of that room looking like mice.

From the ashes emerged a new hope. A husky evangelical from the Shire. What we ended up with was somewhere between the elite Queen's English aristocrat from Sydney's Eastern Suburbs, and the Human Rights-violating former highway cop from North Brissy.

How good.

Peter Dutton Divides His Soul Into Seven Horcruxes As He Makes Move On Liberal Leadership

WITH CONSERVATIVE commentators backing Peter Dutton as the next Prime Minister, it has been revealed today that the Minister for Immigration has divided what remains of his soul into seven fragmented policies to be spread across seven factions within the Australian Liberal Party.

The fragments, known as 'horcruxes', will be hidden in the disguise of policies aimed at not allowing brown people to live in Australia – a constant, but less talked about, sentiment that remains hidden within both sides of federal politics – and one that Dutton has been familiar with for many years.

As outlined in popular Anglo-Celtic folklore, a horcrux is an object in which a Dark wizard or witch has hidden a fragment of his or her soul for the purpose of attaining political immortality. Horcruxes can only be created after committing murder, the supreme act of evil, or allowing people to self-immolate.

With polls sliding, and political commentators gearing up for yet another leadership spill, it is believed that the former Brisbane cop and man who boycotted the national apology to the Stolen Generations, is backing himself as the champion of Australian purity, to possibly take over from Malcolm Turnbull in a desperate bid to remain on $200,000 a year.

When asked if he was worried about being taken out by younger political rivals, Dutton is quoted as saying, 'There are alleged facts that are being put forward by some of the advocates which are patently incorrect, if not fabricated.'

He then went on to point out that innumerate and illiterate refugees could take Australian jobs that Australians don't want to have, before making a cheap shot at the Australian public broadcaster.

Horcruxes can only be created after committing murder, the supreme act of evil, or allowing people to self-immolate.

Turnbull's Leather Jacket Makes Fresh Appearance In Last-Ditch Effort To Prevent Spill

THE PRIME MINISTER used a hot cloth this morning to wipe the mould off his famous leather jacket in a last-ditch effort to prevent an almost unpreventable leadership spill this week.

Though nobody is expected to stand against Malcolm Turnbull should a spill be called from the back bench, the re-emergence of the jacket has some commentators feeling this might spell the end.

But the Member for Wentworth has dispelled the notion, telling journalists this morning in Sydney that he felt a chill in the air and simply reached for an old favourite.

'Ah yes,' he said as an ABC journalist in board shorts and no shirt held his phone by his head.

'Glad to see you've noticed the leather jacket, it's one of my autumn staples. But back to the issue at hand, the 30 Newspoll business is regrettable but not indicative that this government is in trouble. The fact remains that I'm the best leader the LNP has and a far more palatable alternative to William Shorten.

'However, I urge voters to remember why they saw me as an alternative to begin with. Remember the leather jacket, remember me schooling Tony Jones repeatedly on live national television. Remember me as the self-made millionaire with a proven track record of fiscal responsibility.'

Local LNP voters, however, told *The Advocate* that the leather jacket is a distant memory and just because he's wearing it again doesn't mean they'll vote for him again.

'I'd consider it,' said one small business owner. 'Then again, I've got as much faith in the political system in this country as I do in a Michael Clarke return to the Test arena. I'd vote for Albo, though.'

More to come.

Dutton Says He Hasn't Felt This Powerful Since He Was Holding A Radar Gun On The Bruce Highway

SENIOR COALITION FIGURES are trying to contain the rumours that everything has fallen to shit since they all arrived back in parliament last week.

Cabinet Minister Christopher Pyne has rejected a suggestion that Home Affairs Minister Peter Dutton could be considering a leadership tilt, as was suggested by Ray Hadley last week in an attempt to change the subject from his police officer son's cocaine habit.

The Daily Telegraph newspaper, who are also keen to see Turnbull replaced by a scarier conservative, reported that Mr Dutton was being urged to 'seize the leadership from Malcolm Turnbull within weeks on a policy platform of lower immigration and cheaper energy bills'.

Speaking to *The Betoota Advocate* today, the Member for Dickson, Peter Dutton, says he hasn't felt this kind of absolute power since he was a highway cop in Brisbane's northside.

'It was a feeling I never thought I'd experience again,' he told our reporters. 'Not even after being given the right to decide which asylum seekers live or die did I feel this kind of all-encompassing power,' he said.

'But right now, with an entire government waiting on my every word . . . It takes me back to when I was pointing a radar gun at poor commuters rushing to work on the Bruce Highway. Watching someone self-immolate in one of your detention centres is one thing, but to watch a man as wealthy and well spoken as Malcolm Turnbull kneel before you in complete vulnerability. This is the shit that makes me feel alive.'

When asked if he was actually going to have a crack at leadership, Peter Dutton immediately questioned our reporter on whether or not they'd been drinking, before demanding to see some ID.

> *'Watching someone self-immolate in one of your detention centres is one thing, but to watch a man as wealthy and well spoken as Malcolm Turnbull kneel before you in complete vulnerability. This is the shit that makes me feel alive.'*

Turnbull Seen Cartwheeling Down Parliament Hill After Dutton Tells Him To

MOMENTS AFTER the Prime Minister and the Minister for Energy and Environment, Josh Frydenberg, hosted a press conference in Canberra this morning, Malcolm Turnbull was seen doing cartwheels down Parliament Hill while Tony Abbott and Peter Dutton looked on.

'Do a somersault this time!' yelled Dutton as a breathless Prime Minister trudged back up the hill.

Earlier this year, fencing was installed at the bottom of the hill to stop people from walking over Australia's highest temple – but it's still largely within view from the bottom.

'Okay. Is there anything else you want me to do?' asked Turnbull.

Abbott laughed and said no.

All of a sudden, Scott Morrison came bounding out from the fire escape door and said that Barnaby had a good idea.

'Hey, Malcolm!' said Morrison. 'Go down the hill in your kayak! The Nats are carrying it up the stairs now.'

The Prime Minister sighed and agreed. 'Okay.'

With a great echoing, earth-shattering clunk, the kayak appeared atop Parliament Hill from the fire escape door.

Barnaby Joyce, with his tie tangled loosely around his second button, dragged it over to the edge of the hill and threw the Prime Minister's own carbon-fibre oar at him.

'There you go, mate.'

As our nation's leader tucked himself into the kayak and prepared

himself for what could be the wildest ride of his life, he turned and looked up at the God Squad holding the country to ransom and said:

'If I do this, you've got to let me take the party to the next election.'

Morrison, Dutton and Barnaby laughed.

'We know we're fucked but you're the dickhead about to go down a hill in a fucking canoe!' said Joyce.

More to come.

> *'Do a somersault this time!' yelled Dutton as a breathless Prime Minister trudged back up the hill.*

Liberal Back-benchers Terrified They Might Have To Send Their Kids To Local Public Schools

IT CAN BE CONFIRMED today that the fear of God is in the heart of the Liberal Party backbenchers.

The motley crew of middle-aged white men and a few white women are freaking out that if things keep going the way they are, their children may have to pay the ultimate price.

The ultimate price being that they might be forced to attend the grubby local public schools with all the ragtag snotty working-class kids in their electorate.

With the leadership of the Coalition in disarray, and things looking dicey for a lot of MPs at the next election, *The Advocate* has exclusively been informed that a high number of Libs and Nats are willing to do whatever it takes to stay in power.

One backbencher, who requested anonymity, explained that they have come together this afternoon to try and figure out the best way to hold on to their jobs. Sitting in the beer garden of The Snouts in the Trough pub down in the nation's capital, our source said: 'Dutton, Turnbull, Morrison? None of us really give a fuck who is in charge, as long as they win the next election and we get to hold on to our seats.'

'Policy is great in practice and all, but at the end of the day we have to have our priorities right, and that's keeping our kids away from polo shirt–style uniforms and rugby league,' he said.

'So we had a meeting today to try and figure out who is going to be the most electable leader going forward,' he said, before leaving a half-finished glass of pinot noir at the table and telling us he had to go.

'No one is thinking about our welfare. We've got bills and big houses and lifestyles we have become accustomed to. I'm not going to get a real job,' said another backbencher.

More to come.

The motley crew of middle-aged white men and a few white women are freaking out that if things keep going the way they are, their children may have to pay the ultimate price.

'Those Who Are Worried About The Environment Are Just Going To Have To Shut The Fuck Up For Now'

IN THE FACE OF what looks like a very real threat to his leadership, Malcolm Turnbull has today announced plans to remove Paris climate change targets from the National Energy Guarantee in his second policy reset in four days.

The revised scheme will not stipulate a 26 per cent cut to greenhouse gas emissions in either legislation or regulation under changes aimed at keeping nameless backbenchers happy by effectively denying the fact that humans are responsible for any form of environmental damage.

'Those of you who are worried about the environment are just going to have to shut the fuck up for now.'

Asked whether his leadership was under threat, the Prime Minister replied: 'I enjoy the confidence of the cabinet and my party room.'

When asked if he thinks that he might be compromising a bit too much to maintain his position as the most powerful man in Australia, Turnbull responded as honestly as he could.

'Grow a set, you lot. Don't underestimate the erratic behaviour of backbenchers you've never heard of when faced with the possibility of losing their seats due to manipulated power prices, and then being forced to find another job that pays a lot less than $150K per year without perks. It's up to me to control the narrative.

And I believe blaming climate scientists for power prices is the easiest option, and by far the most popular opinion in my party room.'

Turnbull paused briefly and sighed.

'Look, it's either me or Dutton,' he said. 'No one wants to see members of our Muslim community wearing patches on their sleeves.'

> *'Look, it's either me or Dutton,' he said. 'No one wants to see members of our Muslim community wearing patches on their sleeves.'*

'This Is What Happens When You Put Scientists And Human Compassion Before The Party'

TONY ABBOTT HAS TODAY held a press conference, in front of the select few journalists he doesn't believe have a left-wing agenda, to recap on today's events in Canberra.

This follows the news that Malcolm Turnbull has only just beaten Peter Dutton 48–35 in a snap Liberal leadership spill. The Prime Minister forced his rival to show his hand by declaring all leadership positions vacant as soon as the party room meeting started this morning.

Mr Turnbull won the vote and his deputy Julie Bishop was the only candidate to stand for her role. But the result is so narrow it is set to create ongoing problems for the government, and the fact that nearly half the party favour the Minister for Home Affairs is a fair indicator of a definite loss at the next federal election.

Mr Dutton has since volunteered his resignation from the cabinet, and will remain on the back bench for the next couple of months where he will throw peanuts at the Prime Minister until it is time for another spill, which he will most likely win.

Speaking to Sky News, 2GB and *The Daily Telegraph* today at an invitation-only press conference, Tony Abbott says this is what happens when a man that he has a personal vendetta against decides to maybe consider that the multinational mining companies that pay lobbyists millions to take him to lunch could be responsible for damaging the environment.

As well as the whole gay marriage thing, and all this talk of multiculturalism.

'These polls suggest that me and some of my other nameless backbench colleagues might lose our seats at

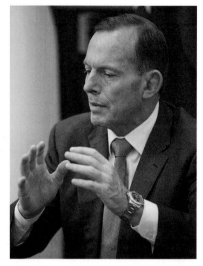

the next election,' he said. 'That's our salaries on the line, mate. This is why Dutton looks like a good option. Because we don't understand the 24-hour news cycle and we hate that he vaguely validates the research of independent scientists who are working to save the Great Barrier Reef. Or the human rights lawyers telling us that what is happening on Nauru is cruel. This is where he went wrong.'

Turnbull Shocks Cabinet And Plays Hidden Immunity Idol

JUST WHEN YOU THOUGHT the fiasco in Canberra couldn't get any more ludicrous, Malcolm Turnbull has blown things up even more.

The seemingly on-the-way-out-the-door Prime Minister has shocked his cabinet, the nation's journalists and his combatants this afternoon by playing an immunity idol necklace.

The immunity idol necklace, according to popular cult reality TV series *Survivor*, grants an individual safety from being kicked out of 'the game', which in the current case is federal politics.

It is not yet known how Turnbull came across the necklace, or how long he has had it in his possession, but some believe it may have been linked to his work on Peter Dutton's eligibility to sit in parliament under Section 44.

Likely facing tribal council tomorrow at 1 pm, the necklace could be an invaluable asset to the former merchant banker-cum-politician.

The tribal council, or Liberal leadership meeting, looks set to go ahead tomorrow after the number of signatures on a petition to call a meeting and force a spill motion grows.

However, with the Prime Minister now in possession of an immunity necklace, it remains to be seen what will be happening in terms of leadership of the party over the next few weeks.

With parliament set to break for two weeks, while the Coalition politicians who've blown the place up take a holiday, Turnbull may have just done enough to hold his place in the tribe for now.

Regardless of the outcome, it looks to be a move that could go down in *Survivor*, and political, history.

More to come.

The Bachelor Ratings Crash As Federal Politics Provides More Irrational Conflict And Petty Drama

IT WAS A BAD NIGHT for soon-to-be former Prime Minister Malcolm Turnbull and an even worse one for Channel Ten.

With the nation's attention being held to ransom by the Coalition Government's leadership debacle, one of the station's flagship reality TV programs suffered a massive hit.

The much hyped and anticipated season of *The Bachelor*, featuring the most ockered-up version of Nick 'the Honey Badger' Cummins, had pulled huge numbers last week, averaging 1.25 million viewers on its launch night.

However, the numbers took a big whack last night as the nation's viewers decided more irrational conflict and petty drama could be found on the nation's news channels, with ABC News 24 drawing large numbers.

Channel Ten's Head of Programming Hugh Burke told *The Advocate* that if things keep going the way they are, they are just going to pull tonight's episode.

'It will be pointless putting it on the air. No one will be watching. We will just save it till next week when all these pollies go on holiday.'

Local *Bachelor* fan Alison Little told *The Advocate* that she knew the news channels were the place to be for gossiping, blow-ups and mindless drama.

'Look, I love watching the Bachie in order to see wanna-be-famous Insta-models with lip filler tee off on each other over the most nonsensical things, but I knew it wouldn't compare to what's going on down in the bush capital,' she explained. 'It's so good. Embarrassing for us as a country but still so good. It's like they don't even care about running the country anymore, they just want to have tiffs about whose side they are on.

'You know what they should do? They should get Keira down there! That would really spice things up.' Little laughed.

Can You Useless Fucks Actually Do Some Work? Asks Nation

Rich White Dude From Sydney's Eastern Suburbs Replaces Rich White Dude From Sydney's Eastern Suburbs As PM

IN BREAKING NEWS out of the nation's capital, a rich white dude from Sydney has replaced another rich white dude from Sydney as the Prime Minister.

After an incredible week in the bush capital, a rich white man named Scott Morrison has replaced Malcolm Turnbull as the Prime Minister of Australia today.

This comes after Scott Morrison stormed home late to pip Peter Dutton and Julie Bishop in the leadership ballot and become the leader of the Liberal Party and the country.

It can be confirmed that Tony Abbott and Peter Dutton have fucked up the numbers and misjudged their support base in pushing for a second spill which has sensationally allowed the party leadership to be pinched from under their noses.

With many in Dutton's camp assuming it a done deal after forcing Turnbull's ministers to resign and pushing for a leadership challenge, the conservative right-wingers have been left crushed by the decision today.

And, in even more sensational news, a rich white woman has been replaced by a rich white man for the Deputy Prime Ministership, with Josh Frydenberg taking over from Julie Bishop.

Parliament House Maintenance Worker Sent To Check On Revolving Door To PM's Office

FOLLOWING THE NEWS of a change of leadership in the Australian Liberal Party, the maintenance and groundskeeping department of Parliament House have sent their best and brightest revolving-door repairman to check up on the state of the entry to the Prime Minister's office.

While the rest of the public servants in Parliament House rush to destroy the Australian Government in a desperate attempt to save their cushy salaries and pensions, the maintenance staff are getting on with the job.

When asked if he reckons the door would be able to withstand this week's leadership crisis and the subsequent re-election of the Labor Party, the revolving-door specialist, Blake Griffin, had this to say:

'Yep.'

Taking a close look at the turning mechanism he added, 'She's looking good. This bad boy should be able to handle two new governments over the next six months. I reckon even the big rig ScoMo could glide through here. Maybe even Albo. But I'll need to come back for another check before then.'

> *'I reckon even the big rig ScoMo could glide through here. Maybe even Albo.'*

Malcolm Turnbull Quits Parliament And Boards One-Way Flight To Cayman Islands

DEPARTING PRIME MINISTER Malcolm Turnbull has thrown the towel in today, announcing that he is quitting parliament, and has called the second leadership spill this week.

After digging his heels in for most of the week, Turnbull finally called the meeting to decide the next Prime Minister of the country, after receiving a letter with 43 signatures on it asking for the conference.

The meeting will feature a leadership spill, with Julie Bishop, Peter Dutton and Scott Morrison all throwing their hats in the ring for the top gong.

It can now be confirmed that Turnbull has sensationally announced that he will be quitting parliament, effective immediately, to head to the Caymans.

In an exclusive interview with *The Advocate* over the phone a short time ago, outgoing Prime Minister Turnbull revealed to us that he is about to get on a one-way flight to the Cayman Islands.

'Yeah, I'm done. Fuck this, I'm out of here. I'm not hanging around to serve under a highway cop who has got the elocution of a highway cop,' Turnbull said over the phone.

'Besides, all my bank accounts and finances are set up over in the Caymans, so it's the perfect fit. I'll head over there, lay low for a year or so, kick the feet up, and think about heading back to Wall Street to ply my trade. A private jet is waiting for me and I'll be heading out of Sydney this afternoon. Enjoy the next few months. Bye bye,' he said before the line went dead.

More to come.

He-Who-Must-Not-Be-Named-Prime-Minister Retreats Back Into The Darkness After Defeat

THE ASPIRATIONAL FORMER Home Affairs Minister has retreated back into the shadows of the Liberal Party after a crushing defeat yesterday.

The ex-Queensland cop is licking his wounds after a demoralising loss in yesterday's leadership spill.

The Dark Lord of Nauru had the top job pinched from under his nose by Scott Morrison after many long months of hard work destabilising the party he is supposed to serve.

The Betoota Advocate can confirm that He-Who-Must-Not-Be-Named has shrunk back into the darkest depths of the Liberal Party to plot what will most likely be another assault with his boss Tony Abbott.

With little to no regard for the people who elected him to the parliament, or the people of Australia generally, the man who walked out on the nation's apology to the Stolen Generations is trying to figure out where to from here.

After tirelessly pushing for a Home Affairs Ministry, the most powerful ministry created in the history of this country, the ex-copper threw it all away for a chance to have a run at the top gig.

With ScoMo and his allies promising not to reward the behaviour of the Dark Lord, Abbott and their friends, it remains to be seen whether he will be able to get back into a position where he can deny asylum-seeking children urgent medical attention again.

More to come.

The Dark Lord of Nauru had the top job pinched from under his nose by Scott Morrison after many long months of hard work destabilising the party he is supposed to serve.

Abbott Family Decide It Might Be Time To Put Dad Into A Home

THE ABBOTT FAMILY has today conceded that it might be time to face reality.

Living on Sydney's leafy north shore, the family made up of Tony's wife, three daughters and sister have had a hard chat today.

After his constant sniping and efforts to sculpt the Liberal Party into a mould of his making, Abbott has been left crushed today as his puppet and stooge Peter Dutton lost the leadership ballot.

So as a result, the family of the Chief White Ant of the Liberal Party

have come together for a round table of sorts, to try and figure out what to do with him.

The Betoota Advocate can exclusively reveal that the consensus reached between the members of the Abbott family is that Tony should be taken and admitted to a nearby aged care facility down the road in Belrose.

Speaking collectively they told us that 'Dad' has done his dash, and as much as they would love to have him around the home, the best place for him would be a nearby nursing home.

'Poor Tony. As I'm sure many of your readers are aware, he has become senile, and it's not safe for him to look after himself in public,' they said to our reporters.

'So we have made the decision to tell him it's time to head up to the oldies' home.'

The family said that they would be

sure to visit him regularly and make sure he was as comfortable as possible.

'I think we are going to take him to the final Sea Eagles game of the season, so when they get the spoon, he will be so broken that he might just agree to it and make things easy.

'But knowing Tony, he never does. So let's see how it goes.'

> *'Poor Tony. As I'm sure many of your readers are aware, he has become senile, and it's not safe for him to look after himself in public.'*

Liberals Urge Dutton To Call Literacy Numeracy Hotline After Inability To Count Lets Him Down

THE HEAVYWEIGHTS in the Liberal Party have sat Peter Dutton down today.

After the border cop from Queensland brought the party to its knees last week, the powers that be decided it was time to have a word to the rogue MP.

The President of The Liberal Party Nick Greiner called Dutton into his office this morning.

'One Three Double Ohhh, Six Triple Fiveeee Ohhhh Six,' he sang to the Home Affairs Minister as he walked into the office.

Greiner then proceeded to walk Dutton through some pamphlets he had obtained earlier and asked the aspiring leader to please call the National Reading and Writing Hotline to sort out his numerical illiteracy.

'After your inability to count made our entire party look like fools last week, we have made the executive decision that you need to work on that area, okay?' he said to Dutton.

Greiner was of course referring to Dutton and his supporters butchering the maths on the number of people who supported him in making a leadership tilt.

Greiner said to us: 'Look, Pete means well, and the nature of the beast nowadays seems to be that you don't wait for power anymore, you just agitate for a few months and then have a big run at it.

'But if Pete, or anyone else for that matter, wants to cause a fuss and try and wrestle the top job off someone, he has to be able to count at a high enough level to make sure that it doesn't come back to bite him, and us.'

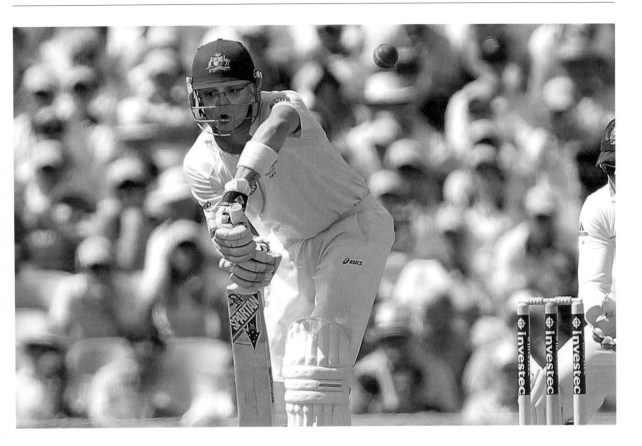

Liberal Party Sends In Scott Morrison As Nightwatchman

THE LIBERAL PARTY OF AUSTRALIA has today sensationally announced that they will be sending in former Treasurer Scott Morrison as their nightwatchman.

A nightwatchman is a term that comes from the sport of cricket and can be described as a lower-order batsman who comes in to bat higher up the order than usual, near the end of the day's play.

With the Liberal Party's top order performing a spectacular collapse over the last few years, a collapse that even the Australian Cricket team could be proud of, they have been forced to send the man now dubbed 'ScoMo' in to bat.

With wickets crumbling, and the test match known as federal politics nearing its end as an election looms, the powerbrokers in the Liberal Party have decided that Scott Morrison was the best lower-order batsman to stave off the slow to medium pace bowling of the Labor Party.

Although unaware he was being sent out to the middle until just a couple of days ago, Scott Morrison will have to do his best to try and survive in what will most likely be a vain attempt at saving the game.

Speaking exclusively to *The Advocate* just moments before heading out to bat today, Morrison told us that the tap on the shoulder came as a bit of a surprise.

'Yeah, I had my feet up in the sheds,' Morrison said whilst toying with his protective gear. 'And then I got told that I've got to go out there and try and block it out and try and save things.

'I mean, it's a shit job, but at least their bowlers have got fuck-all zip. So let's see how we go,' he said before trudging off to the wicket.

NIGHTWATCHMAN

VS

BRADBURY SHORTEN

It was the unwinnable election for the Coalition, their brand was toxic. For the ALP, it was an election they couldn't lose, their brand slightly less toxic. The polls, the gurus and every other half-pissed political genius on election night could only see one outcome.

There was one aspect of the election that most Australians failed to see. It wasn't a contest between the incumbent Coalition government and their Labor opposition, it was a contest between two men.

The Nightwatchman and Bradbury Shorten.

After the binning of Malcolm, people expected the Liberal Party to be whipped by the very people who voted them in. They were now no better than Labor. The internal squabbling, the egos, the sheer ineptitude to govern. The Liberals were putting them before anyone else. There was anger and disappointment. They needed to go.

When Scott Morrison unexpectedly won the second leadership spill after Malcolm resigned, nobody gave him a chance. Bradbury Shorten was already browsing the IKEA website for Lodge furnishings.

Thus, he became the Nightwatchman. A player whose only job was to usher the government to an election loss – then go quietly into the night. His innings was meant to protect the more powerful, long-game players in the party.

However, as the events of 2019 progressed, his innings blossomed from a run-of-the-mill Shane Warne after-tea innings to protect the wicket of Ricky Ponting to a full-on Jason Gillespie double-tonne in Bangladesh in his last ever Test match.

And Bradbury Shorten, well, turns out he was coming first in the race to The Lodge and got taken out by the bloke coming second. He, along with Clive and the other election losers, crashed into the sidewall and could only watch as the man who everybody wrote off coasted to an easy election win.

Sometimes, all you can do is laugh.

Reporters At Shorten's Press Conference Distracted By Paint Drying On Wall Behind Him

BILL SHORTEN has had to interrupt reporters at a press conference this afternoon in an awkward state of affairs.

The Opposition Leader was talking about how slightly different his approach to the budget would have been in an address to a room of reporters from some of the major media outlets, as well as our own Channel Country publication.

However, after a few minutes, Shorten and his advisors noticed that the entire cohort of journos had completely drifted off.

'Hey, did you hear what I just said?

You, from Channel Seven? Are you listening?' he asked frustratedly.

After some dozy nods and awkward glances around the room, Shorten asked if anyone had any questions for him.

'You guys got any questions? Anything? You can ask me whatever you want. I swear. Even about some of the shit I've done in my union capacity,' he said.

'Beaconsfield? Chloe? . . . Fuck youse.'

The Advocate can confirm that everyone in the room, including our very own junior reporters, had lost

track of the presser because they had become distracted by some paint drying on a wall behind the leader of the ALP.

'Yeah, they've put some glossy paint there on the back, sort of behind Bill, and it looks pretty fresh but then it did seem to be drying, so I just got caught up in analysing that whole process, you know,' said one journo who asked to remain anonymous.

'I was initially counting the number of square panels on the lectern when he started, but the paint eventually got the better of me,' the journalist said.

Bill Shorten Begins Studying Videos Of Steven Bradbury's 2002 Olympic Gold Medal Win

BILL SHORTEN has today spent a few hours doing some in-depth research on how to perfect his skate home to the 2019 Prime Ministership.

This comes after the Liberal Party rolled their leader again, after months of very public infighting and bickering.

With Scott Morrison now at the helm after succeeding Malcom Turnbull as Prime Minister, Shorten has reportedly spent the better part of a day watching Steven Bradbury skate home to a gold medal.

Watching the famous win from a number of different angles, in slow motion, and hyper-zoomed, Shorten said he is confident he can emulate the Australian icon, by languishing in the background only to have everyone fall over in front of him.

Shorten then said he just can't believe the sure bet he's been handed, and has decided to just shut the fuck up and smile until he is handed the role of Prime Minister at the next federal election.

'Sounds like a good idea to me,' Shorten said to reporters today. 'I'm not going to say or do anything until after the election. I've been studying videos of Steven Bradbury's 2002 gold medal win at the Salt Lake City Winter Olympics all morning. This election will be quite possibly the only other example of someone actually winning because of a tortoise and hare–type competitive edge.'

Labor Party Calls Emergency Meeting To Discuss How They Can Still Fuck This Up

OPPOSITION LEADER Bill Shorten has called his team into a huddle today.

The Australian Labor Party, looking for all money like they will shit this weekend, have come together to try and figure out how it could possibly go wrong.

With the Coalition Government in tatters, after leadership challenges and ministerial resignations, political commentators have earmarked the ALP as the short odds favourites to storm home and win the election.

However, as in sport, with Bill Shorten at the helm, nothing is a given.

Blessed by the fallout from the leadership calamities before him, Bill Shorten looks to have cemented his place at the head of the ALP table, and has called in his MPs for a conference.

'Okay, so things are going swimmingly for us,' Shorten reportedly addressed the group with a beaming grin on his face. 'Is there any way we can still fuck this one-horse race up?'

At which point a few ministers pointed out that the only way it could all go pear-shaped is if Shorten decided to 'get on the front foot'.

'Please, Bill, just shut up. Don't say anything. Just smile and nod, and allow the Libs to keep letting rounds off into their feet. They will win it for us,' one of the MPs said.

Shorten agreed to keep quiet for the sake of the party.

'I haven't really got anything to say anyway,' he laughed. 'They haven't really been saying much about policy or anything, so I can't just say the opposite of what they say.'

More to come.

'Please, Bill, just shut up. Don't say anything. Just smile and nod, and allow the Libs to keep letting rounds off into their feet. They will win it for us.'

ScoMo Ashamedly Admits He Isn't 'Turnbull Rich' When Asked If He'll Forgo The Salary

THE NATION'S NEWEST Prime Minister Scott Morrison was forced to concede today.

Fielding questions about his newfound role, the rich white man from Sydney had to admit that, while he is rich, he isn't 'Turnbull rich'.

The admission came after we questioned the man being dubbed 'ScoMo' about whether he would be pulling 'a Turnbull' and donating his salary, rather than pocketing it, like all of the nation's other high-paid public servants.

Turnbull made seemingly few headlines when he announced that he would be donating his parliamentary salary to charity, in a show of his intentions in terms of the role.

However, ScoMo told us that while he is reasonably well off, he doesn't think he is well off enough to be running the country pro bono.

'Good on Malcolm, you know, but it's a different kettle of fish for me. Malcolm was a merchant banker, a high-flying barrister and a well-regarded legal counsel. He is worth a lot of money. He is elite-level rich,' Morrison said.

The former Immigration Minister explained to us that while he grew up in the well-to-do electorate of Wentworth, and has been a bureaucrat his whole life, he doesn't consider himself on that level.

'I'm just public-servant rich, which is certainly not rich enough to be turning your nose up at half a mill,' Morrison said.

'In my mind anyway.'

More to come.

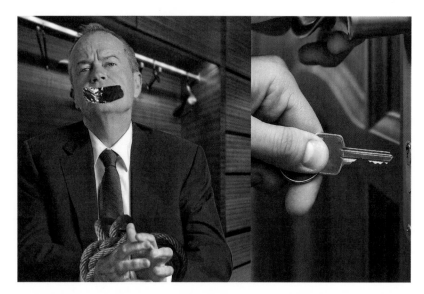

Labor Party Powerbrokers Lock Bill Shorten Away Until Election

KINGMAKERS AND FACTIONAL heavyweights within the Australian Labor Party have pulled the trigger this morning.

It can be confirmed that the powerbrokers in the Labor Party have in fact locked their leader, Bill Shorten, away for the foreseeable future.

This comes after analysts and commentators around the country have concluded that the next election should be 'unlosable' for the ALP.

The continued fallout from the leadership shambles in the Liberal Party has seemingly handed the opposition the election in gift wrapping. However, the heavies within the party, who have been around long enough to remember Mark Latham shitting the bed, told *The Advocate* that there is 'no such thing as a sure thing'.

The source, who requested anonymity, told us that after a snap conference this morning it was decided that Bill Shorten should be locked away, for now.

'We just can't risk him going out and speaking, and doing things, and ruining our chances of winning an election that we "can't lose,"' the source explained. 'So poor old Bill got a knock on the door after he got dressed, and we've stashed him away in a secure location.

'Don't worry. He is okay. He has food and water. Just no access to the outside world. We can't have another Latham-style handshake debacle, can we?' the source said. 'It's for his own good. He will thank us down the track.'

More to come.

Out Of Control Bin Fire Somehow Polling Better Than Bill Shorten As Preferred Prime Minister

It is not yet known why the stinky, smoky pile of burning trash is even being considered as a Prime Minister, while emergency workers unsuccessfully attempt to quell the flames by pouring petrol on it.

A BLAZING PILE OF RUBBISH has today increased its two-party-preferred vote by 3 per cent in the latest Newspoll, shooting past Labor's previous election-winning lead in the wake of the Liberal leadership spill.

It is not yet known why the stinky, smoky pile of burning trash is even being considered as a candidate for Prime Minister, while emergency workers unsuccessfully attempt to quell the flames by pouring petrol on it.

One month after a toxic three-way leadership contest flipped Australia's Prime Minister for the third time since Labor was voted out in 2013, it appears that an out-of-control bin fire has boosted its primary vote by 3 per cent to 36 per cent and now sits behind Labor, 46 per cent to 54 per cent in two-party-preferred terms.

The result represents a 4.4 per cent swing to Labor since the 2016 election, which would lead to the government losing up to 20 seats if replicated in a general election, but it is the first positive movement towards the disgustingly pungent and flat-out concerning skip bin full of fiery trash in some time.

When asked for comment on the worrying poll numbers, Bill Shorten was still talking about the Fatman Scoop video, as it appears to be the only thing that he can honestly say he wouldn't have done as Prime Minister.

It appears that an out-of-control bin fire has boosted its primary vote by 3 per cent to 36 per cent and now sits behind Labor, 46 per cent to 54 per cent in two-party-preferred terms.

ScoMo Still Yet To Be Called Out For Giving Himself A Nickname

ALTHOUGH PRIME MINISTER of Australia and professional seat warmer Scott Morrison has been the nation's leader since August 2018, the nation is wondering exactly when he will be called out for giving himself the nickname 'ScoMo'.

Since being sworn in, the PM has received a lot of criticism from the public for his focus on religious discrimination, lack of action on climate change and for being the sort of person who says 'Spendings, thanks' when paying on card, but has managed to dodge criticism relating to the fact that he was definitely the first person to refer to him as 'ScoMo'.

Traditionally used to belittle someone you care about, nicknames can be an essential part of belonging to a group, which is why it seems highly unlikely that a Liberal Prime Minister would have one, let alone one they like and use on social media.

A spokesperson from the PM's office rejects the claims the Member for Cook came up with his own nickname, stating the nickname was 'actually started by someone cool like Banksy or something' and that it was previously 'DJ ScoMo until he left that life behind'.

A source from inside the Liberal Party, Patrick Dutton (real name changed), confirmed Prime Minister Morrison does have a nickname they all use, just never to his face.

'It starts with a C,' stated the featureless whistleblower.

'And it ends with that cunt getting voted out.'

The Nightwatchman Meets With Dizzy Gillespie To Get Some Tips For Upcoming Election Campaign

WITH THE ALP LOOKING a lot like an out-of-form Bangladesh at Chittagong in 2006, the Prime Minister has today met with the only man who can help him bring it home.

This comes after the Nightwatchman flew from a flooded north Queensland to Moscow to meet with President Putin on Monday, in a failed bid to entice Russian hackers to interfere with the imminent Australian federal election.

Putin was unfortunately not very keen on helping the Coalition Government stay in power, even if it meant having unbridled access to sensitive government documents which are already being hacked and accessed by ten-year-olds.

With no luck, the Final Swirl decided to continue his desperate international pre-election campaign in the UK.

Landing in the south-eastern English county of Sussex this afternoon, the Prime Minister was lucky enough to score a meeting with former Australian cricketing superstar Jason 'Dizzy' Gillespie, who is currently head coach of the Sussex Sharks.

'What do you reckon, Dizzy?' asked the Prime Minister, while casually spinning a six-stitcher between his hands.

'You reckon I've got a double tonne in me?'

Dizzy was quick to point out the key to nabbing a double century against a developing side, saying it helps when you're steaming off the back of a shared fourth wicket partnership of 320 runs with Michael Hussey ... And considering the fact that he is almost solely responsible for Malcolm Turnbull being run out, Morrison is unlikely to ever reach the same heights as a nightwatchman.

'No chance mate,' said Dizzy. 'Just wait for daylight to run out and get a job at BHP.'

Morrison, unsatisfied with Gillespie's lack of faith, began rubbing a cough lolly on the side of the ball.

'What are you even doing talking to me anyway?' spat Dizzy. 'I thought you hired Uncle Tony to talk to me on your behalf?'

Putin Politely Declines The Nightwatchman's Request To Interfere In Our Election

THE COALITION GOVERNMENT has today announced that it is now ready to hand over to Labor, after even the Russians have decided against electing it.

This comes after Prime Minister Morrison took an overnight flight to Moscow from Mount Isa on Sunday to meet with President Putin.

'Come on, Vlad, mate,' begged the Nightwatchman. 'You can have free rein on any intel or trade deals. I promise you won't get shirtfronted. Forget about Tony. He's gone. I threw him a hospital pass and now he's out bush getting yelled at by blackfellas.'

President Putin, however, appeared uninterested in Morrison's proposed offer of 'doing what they did for Trump' and interfering in Australia's upcoming federal election.

'Scott, why would I want to inherit your government?' asked Putin. 'If you had your time again, would you choose to inherit this government?'

Morrison paused for a minute, before conceding that the current Australian Liberal Party would probably be harder to manage than the radical Islamist Chechen rebels of the North Caucasus.

'Good point,' said the Nightwatchman. 'But think of all our sensitive government documents you would have access to.'

It is at this point that President Putin began laughing hysterically, before informing Morrison that he already had access to those documents, and that the most recent cyber attack on Parliament House was hacked by his palace gardener's ten-year-old daughter – and has made for some underwhelming bedtime reading.

Morrison paused for a minute, before conceding that the current Australian Liberal Party would probably be harder to manage than the radical Islamist Chechen rebels of the North Caucasus.

The Nightwatchman Pulls Abbott Aside To Ask If He Honestly Has Fucking Rocks In His Head

AFTER A SHOCKING WEEK that has seen the lower-order leader of the Coalition Government attempting to strike in rapidly worsening light, former Prime Minister Tony Abbott has come steaming in like dark clouds from the west.

This comes as the embattled Member for Warringah took to 2GB yesterday to talk about his 'close friend' George Pell, following the public release of the cardinal's guilty verdict on five counts of child sexual abuse.

In a radio interview with Ben Fordham, Abbott actually admitted that he spoke to Pell on Tuesday after his conviction, but refused to say what he had said to the now convicted child molester.

Abbott has previously described Pell as a 'fine man' and a 'fine human being and a great churchman' who may not be 'perfect' – after he was previously found guilty of protecting other paedophiles in the church, namely his old housemate Father Ridsdale.

> *Abbott apologised, but really did want to point out that Pell isn't half as bad as some of the sickos he went through the seminary with.*

When asked his thoughts on the verdict, Abbott described the news as 'devastating'. When asked who was devastated, Abbott made no mention of victims of child abuse in the Catholic Church.

'Certainly [devastating], for the friends of Cardinal Pell, and as you say, I am one. Devastating for all who believe in the Catholic Church, and I'm also one of those.'

It was this bizarre radio interview that has resulted in a reluctant, and furious, lecture from the Caretaker Prime Minister Morrison.

'Hey Tony, got time for a quick chat?' Morrison asked after crossing paths in Canberra yesterday.

'Hey mate, just keen to know, in all honesty, do you have fucking rocks in your head?'

A startled Abbott was quick to point out to his Pentecostal successor, that while, yes, he has suffered mild CTE throughout a lifetime of low-quality rugby union and boxing with English nerds at Oxford, he does in fact have a brain.

Morrison then went on to ask him, 'Well, why the fuck are you going on 2GB for Fordo? You know he's not as safe as Hadley, he'll stitch you up. You flat-out admitted to being a friend and a supporter of a convicted paedophile, you dumb cunt. We'll both be driving trucks in a couple months if you keep this shit up.'

Abbott apologised, but really did want to point out that Pell isn't half as bad as some of the sickos he went through the seminary with.

To make matters worse, the Nightwatchman was again smashed with glare yesterday after another increasingly irrelevant ex-Prime Minister reportedly provided a glowing reference for Pell to the court, praising him as a person of 'high intelligence and exemplary character' – even after knowing about his conviction.

Nightwatchman Asks Michaelia Cash If She Could Organise A Cake For International Women's Day

THERE WAS A CERTAIN DREAD in the air at Parliament House today after the majority of its constituents had to relinquish their dominance for a few hours.

Not wanting to create another media shitstorm, the Nightwatchman got on the front foot and made a thoughtful gesture to one of the only women left on his side of parliament.

'Michaelia, Happy International Women's Day,' said he Nightwatchman. 'I thought it would be a good idea to do something for all of the women here, you know, to show our support.'

At this point Michaelia allowed her mind to wander and imagine a parliament where there was equality.

This mirage was quickly turned to dust as ScoMo revealed what his thoughtful gesture was.

'Do you think you could quickly whip up a cake for everyone?'

ScoMo was met with a completely dumbfounded Cash, and taking note of her reaction he quickly tried to make amends.

'Oh, sorry, of course you don't have time to bake one, you can go and get one from a bakery – I won't tell anyone!'

The Nightwatchman then trotted off, turning around only to tell Ms Cash that he was quite partial to a Black Forest cake.

More to come.

'Oh, sorry, of course you don't have time to bake one, you can go and get one from a bakery – I won't tell anyone!'

Bloke Wearing Sleeveless Puffer Jacket Really Impressed By Federal Budget And ScoMo In General

A LOCAL 20-SOMETHING graduate stockbroker has today called it early that Scott Morrison will win the 2019 federal election.

While speaking to his uninterested mates about last night's Federal Budget, the high-pitched neoliberal expressed the view that last night's budget was very impressive, and so is Scott Morrison, considering what he's been handed, and not to downplay him just yet.

'Just you watch, mate. He'll win this thing. I'm really impressed by him and the other bloke [Josh Frydenberg MP].'

It is not yet clear to the other punters at the Lord Kidman hotel why Hunter Bligh (22) felt the need to ruin a perfectly good piss-up with weird political conversations, but the fact he was wearing a sleeveless puffy jacket with a checked shirt said enough.

The former third XV halfback for one of the most prestigious private schools in western Queensland has paired his 'concrete cowboy' look with a pair of khaki chinos and dark brown dress boots – the type of outfit usually reserved for young Australian men who are confident they will never have to join the military and fight unnecessary wars in the Middle East.

Bligh, who was barely even a teenager when John Howard was voted out of power, has today regurgitated his conservative father's drunken golf rant that suggests the former Prime Minister was the greatest Australian leader in modern history.

'Mate,' he says. 'Easily. You should read his autobiography. It'll really change your view of him.'

While appearing to talk from 'life experience' when discussing trade laws and tax breaks, Hunter is yet to reveal that he still lives at home and refuses to pay rent to his Valium-addled parents because he needs to save for a new start-up idea.

Bligh, who was barely even a teenager when John Howard was voted out of power, has today regurgitated his conservative father's drunken golf rant that suggests the former Prime Minister was the greatest Australian leader in modern history.

Shorten To Remain Undecided On Adani Until He's In Central QLD And There Are No Cameras Around

OPPOSITION LEADER BILL 'BRADBURY' SHORTEN has today confirmed that when it comes to Adani, he will remain as neutral as the nation of Switzerland, until he's in central Queensland and no one's around.

This admission comes this morning after news broke that it is looking ever more likely that the Government will allow a giant multinational company to desecrate Queensland's environment in a perfect example of a political system held to ransom by rampant capitalism.

However, rather than coming out and condemning the Government's support for the Carmichael coalmine which the nation's environmental scientists say is a very bad idea, the leader of the country's Labor Party has refused to comment just yet.

Shorten has confirmed that he won't overturn the Government's decision if he Bradburys his way to power this year, and that he won't be providing his stance on the mine until he is alone with some swing voters in Queensland and the cameras are not rolling.

'I'll be giving comment on this issue that has been running for the last few years in the national spotlight when the time is right and my staffers have figured out where the highest number of votes are,' he said. 'If it becomes an election issue then of course I will just say the opposite of what the Libs are saying, but until then I'm just going to whisper my quiet support to people in marginal electorates that benefit economically in the short term.'

Shorten then checked with his advisors and informed *The Advocate* that that is all he was allowed to say today.

The Nightwatchman Says Aussies Prefer Cars With A Bit Of Grunt Like His 2012 Hyundai Santa Fe

THE NIGHTWATCHMAN has accused Labor of declaring a 'war on the weekend' with its plan for half of all new cars to be electric by 2030, arguing that it is a policy that appears to disrupt the status quo.

This comes as a surprise, given the fact that the moderate Elonmusxuals in the Coalition have championed electric cars for years, and it has been providing concessional loans to help get more on our roads.

Criticism of the 50 per cent target is also at odds with evidence from public servants, who have told Senate Estimates the Coalition has assessed its own target as being between 25 and 50 per cent.

However, as the lower-order leader of the Liberal Party has pointed out, the general public don't know enough about electric cars – so obviously he's going to use this as a hot-button issue and insinuate that every tradie in Australia will have their ute confiscated.

'What Australians have always expressed a preference for is the vehicles that have a bit of grunt and a bit of power, because they like to enjoy the great recreational opportunities that are out there,' he said.

'Like my 2012 Hyundai Santa Fe. It's not exactly a RAV4 but it has the same off-road capabilities, complete with the reliability and slick design that the South Koreans are known for. Jenny rocks the Statesman, but ScoMo, he likes his toys … I'm a bit of a petrolhead, you could say, and I'll be damned if my compact four-by runs off anything but 10 per cent ethanol unleaded!'

'I'm a bit of a petrolhead, you could say, and I'll be damned if my compact four-by runs off anything but 10 per cent ethanol unleaded!'

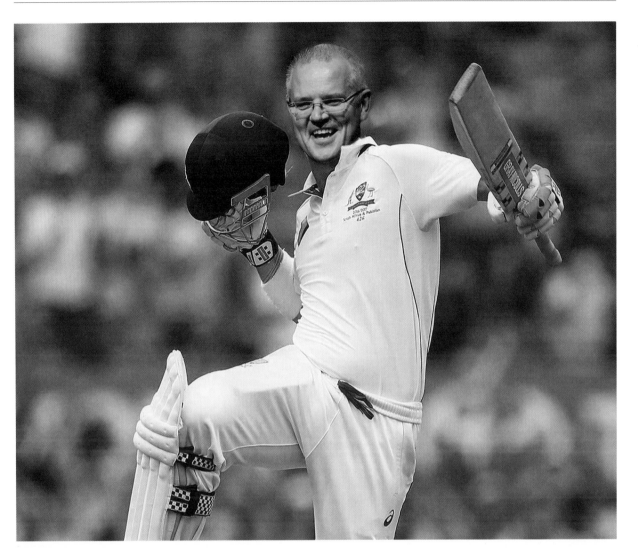

Nightwatchman Finishes The Day Not Out On 201

THE PRIME NIGHTWATCHMAN of Australia has survived to stumps this evening, defying all odds and finishing the day not out on 201.

The Nightwatchman came to the crease some 267 days ago to steady the ship after a top-order collapse that saw team captain Malcolm Turnbull lose his wicket cheaply.

Shortly before stumps this afternoon in Dhaka, Bangladesh was able to break the partnership, sending the Nightwatchman's partner, Uncle Tony X, back to the sheds for 49.

Speaking to *The Advocate*'s cricket correspondent as he took his pads off in the dressing room, the Nightwatchman didn't pull any punches.

'Who's the Nightwatchman now, you fucking cunts?!' he laughed.

This is a developing story.

More to come.

'Who's the Nightwatchman now, you fucking cunts?!' he laughed.

Labor Hires Forensic Cleaners

THE AUSTRALIAN LABOR PARTY has today engaged the services of one of the country's most revered forensic cleaners.

After what can only be described as one of the most horrendous bed-shits in living memory, heavyweights within the party have decided to bring in the big guns to try and clean up the appalling mess.

In what looks like an example of what would happen if someone who had just had an Indian banquet and 11 Crownies got a bout of gastro during their sleep, the party is desperately trying to figure out how they shit the bed so badly.

With the stench from the faeces indicating it may have something to do with a leader who has been unpopular for years, it now looks like the cleaners and the party will have some time to clean up the disgusting mess and reassess where they are at with a long spell on the sidelines ahead.

Speaking to *The Advocate* briefly from inside their HAZMAT suits outside the Labor Party headquarters, one of the cleaners explained they hadn't seen a mess this bad since the Engadine Maccas Incident in 1997.

'Yeah, I was on the scene for the Michael Daley incident earlier this year, and that was nothing compared to this,' he said.

'Fuck, obviously all the ignoring of the leader's unpopularity is part of the mess, and then there's a failure to explain their policies, as well as the Murdoch empire's power and the Australian voters' desire to ensure they benefit as much as financially possible, or are in the position to benefit as much as financially possible from the Liberals' policies if they ever progress from the working class to the middle class and upper class . . .

'Anyway, we've got a lot of work to do, so I best be off,' said the cleaner, trudging off into the disgusting scene.

> *In what looks like an example of what would happen if someone who had just had an Indian banquet and 11 Crownies got a bout of gastro during their sleep, the party is desperately trying to figure out how they shit the bed so badly.*

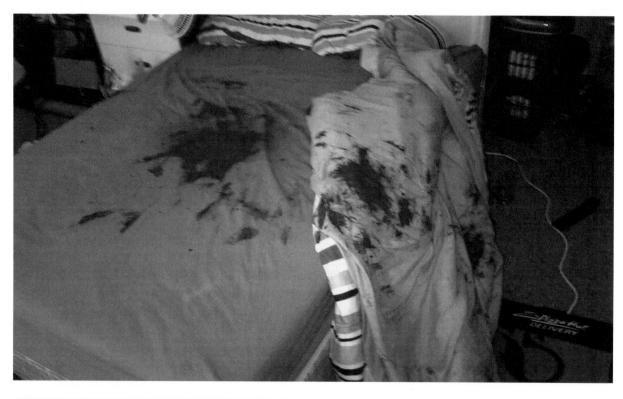

Newtown Girl Whose Mum, Dad, Siblings And All Four Grandparents Voted For ScoMo Says Fuck QLD

BETHANY CUNNINGHAM (23) says she knows it sounds like, kind of harsh, but Queenslanders are just redneck pieces of shit who vote against their own interests because they are racists who aren't very well educated.

The Newtown-based post-grad arts student says she really cannot fathom a population of five million people who could get it so wrong.

'They really fucked it for Labor,' says Bethany, who voted for the Greens on the weekend. 'It's because they are all bogans. I seriously can't believe they voted for ScoMo and his slogans over extremely complex changes to tax legislation.'

However, twenty or so clicks south, deep in the Cook electorate, the rest of the Cunningham tribe have got the Crownies on ice.

'How good!' shouts Bethany's brother Toby, a fridge mechanic from Cronulla.

'How fucken good!' shouts her old man, Hogan, a local tiler turned property investor.

'That fucken good!' shouts her mum, Donna, a well-known local real estate agent.

'About as fucken good as it gets!' shouts Nonno, a fruit truck driver.

With her family eating fresh prawns out of a Styrofoam box and the Crownies and Yellow Tail flowing, Bethany has decided to give this family catch-up a miss and stay put in Sydney's entitlement belt for the weekend. Mainly because she's too sad about the election result.

Unbeknownst to Bethany, or perhaps very well known to Bethany, both sets of her grandparents were handing out Liberal how-to-vote cards over the weekend, after Chris Bowen literally told them not to vote for Labor.

> 'They really fucked it for Labor,' says Bethany, who voted for the Greens on the weekend. 'It's because they are all bogans. I seriously can't believe they voted for ScoMo and his slogans over extremely complex changes to tax legislation.'

In fact, the only other person in Bethany's extended family who didn't vote for the Liberals on the weekend was her cousin Darren from Wollongong – who voted for Clive Palmer because he thought it would be funny.

When asked if she views her entire bloodline in the same light as she views the deplorable Queenslanders who secured Scott Morrison's re-election over the weekend, Bethany says it's different.

'Queenslanders voted for the Liberals because they are racist hillbillies and only care about themselves. My family only voted Liberal because they wanted to protect a tax loophole where people too well-off to need the pension could claim cash refunds for a tax they effectively didn't pay.'

> In fact, the only other person in Bethany's extended family who didn't vote for the Liberals on the weekend was her cousin Darren from Wollongong – who voted for Clive Palmer because he thought it would be funny.

BATTLE OF THE AGES

Starting an intergenerational war between the boomers and their offspring catapulted the Coalition to an election victory in 2019. The real enemy is parliament. The regressive tax policies of the government and Labor's love of rolling over and letting ScoMo scratch their little furry tum-tums has only widened the gap between generations of Australians.

Aside from being the only generation that could've helped prevent the catastrophic changes in climate that will come over the next 50 to 100 years, the boomers have contributed a lot to Australian life.

But it's their continued persecution of freedoms and privileges, often the ones they enjoyed when they were young, that really puts them at odds with the rest of the country.

The boomers voted with their retirement savings in mind at the 2019 election. The millennials voted for someone.

In the middle of all this is Generation X, Australians born in the 70s. Caught between being 'young enough' to work at Triple J and owning a nice enough house within a good walk of their town's central business district.

They will continue to be ignored by boomers, millennials and Canberra until they die. Shrug.

Nevertheless, election wars herein will always include battle, skirmishes and running firefights between the generations so get used to it. It's not going away.

Chances are you're reading this on Christmas Day, or even Father's Day if you're that lucky. You might be a boomer, you might be a gen X ghost, a millennial who's staring down the barrel of dying in a climate disaster or a war with Russia or China – or a gen Z who doesn't really understand anything in this book of unabridged jibberish.

Take a look now at your child or your parents. Give them a good look. Sitting there, enjoying the day. Oblivious for the moment to the horrors of everyday life.

Are they the ones you should be fighting? Or is it Canberra?

What Crisis? How To Buy A Sydney Apartment On A $29,000 Salary

WHAT HOUSING AFFORDABILITY CRISIS? If you're a gen Y having trouble getting into the property market, take a lesson from this 23-year-old.

Charlotte Blakelly-Clapham bought her first property on her 18th birthday – she was ready to go at 17, but wasn't old enough.

The former media student bought the two-bedroom apartment in the working-class Sydney suburb of Balmoral for $1,030,000 with a $130,000 deposit.

But it wasn't easy – she worked at her father's law firm two nights a week since the age of 16, saving most of her pay. That money, combined with savings from her other babysitting job, made up the bulk of her deposit.

'I saved $2,500 – my parents lent me $127,500,' she says.

Ms Blakelly-Clapham says owning a property had been her dream for as long as she could remember.

'It was my goal as a little girl. My parents were always buying property and having fights – I didn't want to be poor my whole life, but I could deal with being unhappy,' she says.

'Using your parents as a bank is the wisest option for gen Yers like me. Most of my friends blow all their money on boys, bars and blow – it's so pathetic. You can get all that by being a little flirty. That's where I save a lot of money. I'm really really happy with what I've done. They've set me up for life.'

Having a goal to work towards from such an early age arguably gave Ms Blakelly-Clapham a head start over her friends, who would spend most of their wage. She was also lucky that her father is Jewish and her mother is Irish Catholic, as both cultures are very generous.

'I spent most of my bat mitzvah money on travel. I adore travelling. Dad was a bit angry when I told him I'd spent nearly all the $400K. Mum had an aneurysm and she hasn't been the same since. But I worked hard when I was a kid to save,' she says.

'I spent my money as well but I was smart with it. I'd always either buy on ASOS or go to Vinnies. Say I earned $600 a week, I'd save $400 and spend $200.'

Knocked down from an initial asking price of $1,100,000, the Balmoral property is now worth more than $1,400,000, and is earning positive rental income.

The part-time law clerk with Minter Ellison still lives with her parents at Clifton Gardens, but is already planning her next investment, and aims to have three by the end of the year.

'We're just weighing up my equity at the moment, but we're looking at either two properties in Bowral or one in Palm Beach,' she says.

Charlotte, who is on a $29,000 salary, is just one of a new generation of property investors. New research has revealed gen Ys are jumping on the property ladder even earlier than other generations.

Her goal is simple. 'I want to retire in my 40s with a positive income,' she says.

'But if that doesn't happen, I can always marry well – I guess?'

> *'We're just weighing up my equity at the moment, but we're looking at either two properties in Bowral or one in Palm Beach,' she says.*

31-Year-Old Unsure If His Alcoholism Is Still Legendary – Or If It's Starting To Get Sad

THERE WAS ONLY ONE wedding invitation on his fridge in December, now there's seven.

It's not because Jack Regent is particularly popular, nor is he being dragged kicking and screaming to them. The 31-year-old has seven wedding invitations on his fridge because he's 31 years old.

But that's not fazing Jack, because he's still a bit of a mad dog. Every wedding he's been to, the boys always look to him to organise the bags of Nosé and some Valium for the next day.

He's a loose unit.

However, as all of his friends begin to settle down around him, the term deposit specialist has started wondering if his hedonism is still legendary – or are his mates starting to feel sorry for him?

'Look, mate. If I was 29 still, I'd still be going to these weddings, getting blind and leaving hotel rooms looking like a painter's radio,' he said. 'But the reality is I'm not getting any younger … and what I do twice a week, half the boys would be lucky to do twice a year now. It's pretty grim. But I'm not sure if it's getting grim for me or getting grim for them. Know what I mean?

'I do get these moments of clarity, like when I'm having nose beers in a nightclub toilet on a Thursday night. Walking out of the cubicle and look at myself in the mirror, I'm like, "What the fuck are you doing with your life? Haven't you called your parents in over a month? You're a fucking monster," but then I just chalk it up to being really high and shrug it off.'

For now, Mr Regent says he's content with being a grub, but looks to try being a coupled man in years to come.

Climate Change No Longer An Issue As Baby Boomers Realise Winter Still Gets A Bit Cold

GILBERT KLOGHEART doesn't know how the world could be heating up if the eastern seaboard has just experienced its coldest weather episode in 20 years.

Despite loud and ghastly shouting matches with his adult children, the 59-year-old remains unswayed on the issue of climate change. Even as the scientific facts and evidence began to mount, Klogheart would often retort in a vulgar manner by pretending to masturbate while blowing a raspberry.

'It's all bullshit,' Klogheart would yell. 'You can't tell me that the world's fucked because it's getting too hot, cunt, it's fucking snowing outside. It's never fucking snowed here before. Forgive me if I'm fucking wrong, but you don't have to be the smartest cunt in the conga line to know it has to be fucking freezing for it to snow. I mean, God strike me down! I don't need these scientists feeding me hot cock. Global warming is bullshit.'

The Advocate was contacted by his son, Elias, who wished to shame his father for his backward attitude towards climate change. We told him not to snitch on his dad and to move out of his house because even his mother agrees that he's a layabout leftie.

'You can't tell me that the world's fucked because it's getting too hot, cunt, it's fucking snowing outside. It's never fucking snowed here before.'

Baby Boomer Who Did LSD Every Weekend In 1969 Sick Of Noise Coming From Local Pub

LOCAL BABY BOOMER Frances Garvey (66) has already called the police 13 times this weekend.

The main issue, Frances says, is that she is having trouble watching her favourite reruns of small-town BBC murder mysteries because of the faint thuds of a vibrant live music venue at the end of her street.

'This is not what I signed up for when I decided to retire in an inner city terrace house,' she says. 'Who do they think they are, playing music at that level, and on a weekend as well. It's just feral. If you want to listen to live music, go to Byron bloody Bay. I'm just waiting for someone to die from getting punched so we can close the place down for good!'

The term 'baby boomers' is used to describe people born during the post–World War II baby boom, approximately between the years 1946 and 1964. This includes people who are between 51 and 70 years old in 2016.

The Australian chapter of the baby boomers have been under fire for attempting to turn the country into a 'perpetual retirement village' with members of generations X and Y citing the lack of nightlife in capital cities and the boomer-centric property bubble edging them out of the same opportunities offered to their parents.

Luckily for Mrs Garvey, and thousands of other baby boomers, the state governments across Australia recognise her struggle.

'I guess I am lucky,' she says. 'The police shut down the party and fined the licensee over $30,000. Rightly so. It's not like when I was younger and we socialised in normal ways. Like listening to Janis Joplin and doing LSD for hours, every weekend.

'Now all I've got to do is figure out how we are going to get them to move the Indigenous community housing down the street. This was not what I had in mind when I bought this place for $11,000 in the 80s. I am a Caucasian post-war Australian. I have never made a compromise in my entire life and I'm not going to start now!'

Unsupervised Boomer Finds Himself Watching SBS Food Again

A BETOOTA GROVE FATHER OF FOUR has been left to his own devices this morning, something that the sexagenarian relishes and enjoys.

Colin Dollarhyde is using the lack of spousal supervision to his advantage, he says, by sitting himself down on his new Koala lounge in front of the 'idiot box'.

In particular, SBS Food.

Speaking a short time ago to *The Advocate* via telephone, the surprisingly virile Gemini said he somehow always ends up enjoying food channels more than others.

'I enjoy watching Nigella,' he said. 'It is much easier to watch than the others. Rick Stein is okay but he looks ill. Bourdain is always great but it makes me sad now. Don't get me started on Jamie Oliver. Honest to Christ, he must live in an alternate universe where things take a quarter of the time to do as they do in our dimension.

'I respect Gordon Ramsay; because I think he'd be able to fuck me up if we ever got into a fight. But yes. Nigella is my favourite. Do you need me to spell it out for you? I don't think so.'

However, Dollarhyde said he can only enjoy these shows unsupervised. He told our reporter that his wife and kids often 'give him stick' for enjoying Nigella's shows as much as he does.

Late last year, Colin said he was caught watching *Nigella's Christmas Special* with his wife and eldest daughter, who both rolled their eyes at him and called him a 'creepy old man'.

'That's the thanks you get for putting a roof over their heads, putting them through two private schools because of their upper-middle-class problems with authority. Putting them through a ceramics course at the tech college because that's their passion. Sometimes I wish I'd voted for Kim Beazley so I'd be poor now. Oh well.'

More to come.

> *'I respect Gordon Ramsay; because I think he'd be able to fuck me up if we ever got into a fight. But yes. Nigella is my favourite. Do you need me to spell it out for you?'*

Little Brother Extra Chirpy At Family Breakfast Because He's Still Very, Very Pissed

WILL HYDE (18) was unable to explain his uncharacteristically talkative mood today as he sat down for Easter Sunday lunch. His mother, Jane, on the other hand, thinks she has a pretty good idea of what might be at play.

'He's still pissed!' proclaimed Jane in that disapproving tone mothers do so well. 'He sat next to that bloody cousin of his, Kurt, at dinner last night.'

Will, who is usually a nervous mute, was more than happy to chew the ear off one of our reporters shortly after lunch finished, talking to us about how his cool older cousin took him out on the piss.

'Haha, how are you guys? Do you want a drink or anything? I'll get back on it when Mum's not looking.'

With Will's slightly altered state, our reporters struggled to keep him on track. However, after a few subtle redirects, they managed to steer him back to the conversation at hand.

'Drinking is pretty cool, have you guys had rum before? How about Baileys?'

The Advocate understands that Will has already messaged his close friends to inform them of his newfound thirst for the Devil's elixir, putting his hand up to be in charge of bringing the rum to their next pre-drinks.

More to come.

Staff Drinks Ruined By Hipster Intern's Revolting Craft Beer Selection

AFTER JUST 35 MINUTES in the pub, every person sitting at the table reserved for *Out Bush* magazine's quarterly staff drinks has decided to pack in.

With what looked to be an endless bar tab, a good crowd of solid drinkers and early dinner out of the way – Managing Director, Ben Bridle, can't understand what went wrong.

'I'd been down the street buying a pack of smokes. By the time I rushed back … I only caught the last of them. I thought we were gonna turn on one. I was paying for everything.'

By the time Mr Bridle had returned from the local convenience store, just about everyone in the office had left the table – leaving only the newly appointed unpaid intern and Sarah from HR.

'Sarah had a very serious look on her face and Jacob [the intern] looked like he was about to cry,' said Bridle. 'Turns out he's fucked everything up after buying the first round. I should have known that he wasn't mature enough to handle the company card.'

It is believed that Jacob the intern (19) was met with severe hostility and disgust by the rest of the office after he decided to buy 12 pints of Phantom Brewers Passionfruit Lager.

'I had to file an incident report with HR. The kid got a very serious warning about forcing personal beliefs onto other staff members,' said a cranky Bridle, who was ready to really turn one on.

'Fuck it, I might go ahead and fire the little prick. It's just not acceptable. I should have left the card with Kev from accounts – he knows a real beer.'

Confused Boomers Clutch Printed-Out Itinerary Hoping It Will Reveal How To Check-In

'WHAT THE FUCK is a self-serve check-in kiosk?' she said.

Graeme Chambers grimaced and thought about throwing his bag down and walking away.

She wasn't helping.

'This is what we get for not flying Qantas! There should be a nice Australian girl at a desk for us to talk to! Instead, we're out here looking like a couple of SHAGS ON A ROCK!'

Both Graeme and his wife of 30 years, Cassowary, were struggling to comprehend the brave new world of air travel today at the Remineko Memorial Airport as they stood by the entrance clutching their travel itinerary – hoping that if they checked it enough times, it would answer their problems.

'You cheap son-of-a-bitch, Graeme! I'd rather backflip into an empty pool than fly Tiger with you again!'

Our reporter, who was checking in nearby, thought about helping them check into their flight.

But after Graeme explained that they'd arrived at the airport six hours early, *The Advocate* decided it'd probably be better off in the long run if they worked it out themselves.

More to come.

First Home Buyers Posing With 'Sold' Sign Acting Like They Had No Help From Parents

A POPULAR YOUNG professional couple has recently taken to social media to show friends, family and casual onlookers that they've recently entered the property market – heralding a new chapter in their lives.

Marcia Sock and Gavin Coolidge, both of Betoota Grove, are the new owners of a handsome four-bedroom home in a quiet cul-de-sac just steps from the homes they grew up in.

According to the pair, they've made many sacrifices to get where they are and that any young person can enter the housing market – provided they're willing to work hard and go without.

'I've effectively given up skiing,' said Gavin, who graduated Deputy Head Prefect from the Whooton Academy – a large publicly funded private school in the heart of town.

'Marcia hasn't taken stress leave for over a year. It's been real ear-to-the-grindstone type slogging that's gotten us to where we are. Haters will say my dad helped me, or Marcia's dad. The simple fact of the matter is that they didn't just give us the money, we actually have to pay our parents back the 40 per cent deposit. So fuck off.'

The selling agent initially told our reporter that the vendor wished to keep the sale price confidential, however, our reporter took him out on the town last night and got the figure out of him.

He said the two-acre property, complete with pool and man cave, sold for close to $2.1 million.

The Advocate reached out to Gavin Coolidge Snr for comment on the matter and received a prompt reply.

'Of course I lent him money to *buy* a house. Almost half a million Australian pesos!' he said. 'I could afford it – and he only earns $70K a year so I had to co-sign the mortgage, too. Marcia's father also chucked in a bit, not as much as me. He's paying for the wedding and six-month honeymoon so it's only fair. We actually played golf a few months ago and the loser had to pay the first kid's private school tuition.

'I won but paid for the drinks afterwards!'

When pushed by our reporter, Gavin Snr conceded that it wouldn't be possible to enter the property market without outside help.

'Well, if you want to live in a nice part of town or in a big city, you'll need help as a young person. Little to no real wage growth, increased living expenses and an overinflated housing market? You don't have a chance. Any young person who's "bought" a nice house in a nice area had help from outside money and if they tell you otherwise, they're full of shit.'

Boomers Welcome Grandchild Into World Who'll Inevitably Die Because Of Their Environmental Vandalism

A SEMI-RETIRED Betoota Grove couple welcomed their first grandchild into the world over the weekend and they've been doting on the little bundle of joy ever since.

Graham and Enola 'Butter' Rogers, both 68, took a break from manhandling their eldest son's baby to speak to *The Advocate* about the joy pulsating throughout their bodies at the moment.

The couple spoke to *The Advocate* on the deck of their eldest child's Betoota Ponds townhouse, which backs onto our reporter's comically appalling abode.

'Little Jessie was born at 3 am on Sunday morning. She was 4125 grams! What a little cannonball!' said Graham.

'We're just so happy,' added Butter.

'Our first grandchild. I'm a grandmother! We've been waiting an age for this. For Graham Jnr to settle down. He's just put a deposit down and now he's got the baby! Just fantastic.'

However, as the bubbly Butter ploughed through a delicious Red Rothmans – she confided in our reporter that she held fears for the future.

'The world is not the same as it was when I was having babies,' she said, coughing. 'You've got unchecked immigration, climate change, antibiotic resistance, the death of bees, permafrost defrosting, the ice caps melting, the list goes on. I hope the next generation has what it takes to solve these problems. The future does fill me with dread! Not that it matters for me. I'll either be in the ground or on someone's mantelpiece in 20 years or so.'

Graham Snr then slid the flyscreen open to join our reporter and Butter out on the deck.

'They'll be right, Butter. They'll be able to fix it with computers. Don't worry yourself like that. It's not our problem.

'We can only love our children and grandchildren as much as we love ourselves.'

More to come.

Baby Boomer Who Made 68 Noise Complaints Over Weekend Detests Nanny-State Plastic Bag Ban

ANDREW HOPKINS, a 67-year-old accountant from Betoota Ponds, has called for a ban.

A ban on 'bans', unless they are things that are ideologically aligned with his worldview like banning the burqa, late-night pub trade or kids from using smartphones.

Hopkins explained that the spread of political correctness has gone too far.

The Ponds resident, who has been vocal in his letters to *The Advocate*'s editor Clancy Overell about the Railway Hotel's noise pollution in his quiet leafy suburb, explained that the recent plastic bag ban was the watershed moment for him.

'That was the moment I knew I had to stand up. The plastic bag ban is environmental symbolism at its very worst,' he said. 'Things are starting to mildly inconvenience me, therefore they should stop immediately. I'm sick to death of it. Everywhere you look these days, the left are clawing away at our freedoms and the things that have made this beautiful country what it is today,' Hopkins said.

'You can't say "mankind" anymore,' continued the father of four who has literally never been pulled up for saying 'mankind', but read it in a News Corp editorial somewhere. 'This country is getting brainwashed by leftist do-gooders who want us to effectively become a Soviet state.'

Hopkins admitted that he does feel a little bit helpless in the battle against political correctness.

'It's hard to know how to be effective as an individual against this vague term for an ideology that is seeping into every aspect of my life,' Hopkins explained. 'So I've just gotta stick to my guns, I guess. Keep posting on Cheryl's and my Facebook wall. It's up to comfortably retired post-war Australians to keep bringing up how bad political correctness is, and keep lecturing my communist children.'

> 'You can't say "mankind" anymore,' continued the father of four who has literally never been pulled up for saying "mankind", but read it in a News Corp editorial somewhere.'

New Baby Boomer–Themed GPS Tells Users How This All Used To Be Bush

THE GLOBAL POSITIONING SYSTEM (GPS) game has received a shake-up this week, with the arrival of the new baby boomer–themed voice navigator.

Pundits, however, are at odds as to whether the new baby boomer (BB) system will help or hinder motorists.

The new program utilises the core data from Google Maps, but has an added feature which includes sometimes confusing directions and whingeing commentary about how different the landscape was in the 80s.

'Essentially, it's just your old man or mother, narrating the journey, with all that stuff about how much quicker everything is with the new roads and bypasses and so on,' said local tech guru and owner of Ted's Tech in the French Quarter, Ted Hamley. 'I'm not sure if it's going to help people or piss them off,' he said.

Hamley said he has been using the GPS for the last couple of weeks and has started to notice a more nuanced and subtle undertone to the commentary.

'I have been picking up little things like whining about how much easier it was for me to buy my car than it was for the narrator to buy their car, and how much easier my life is compared to how theirs was at my age.'

CEO of the new Boomer-themed software company, Bill Forrest, explained to us that the subtle self-righteous undertone was all part of the charm.

'We have designed it so it's exactly like your father or mother is sitting right there with you, asking probing questions, giving last-minute directional instructions and telling you how easy you have got it.'

> 'We have designed it so it's exactly like your father or mother is sitting right there with you, asking probing questions, giving last-minute directional instructions and telling you how easy you have got it.'

Overconfident Intern Forgets Who The Fuck She's Talking To And Signs Off Email With 'Cheers'

LOCAL UNPAID SEAT-FILLING INTERN Jessica Bardon (22) has today shown a little bit too much familiarity within the multinational media company she will never be hired by.

The media time-check and data entry specialist has today shown just how little she cares about a career in this industry, after sending through a rather unprofessional email about an upcoming branding disruption event – a task that has kept her in the office until midnight for the past two weeks.

Her email is as follows:

I have booked the portaloos and food truck to arrive at the edgy warehouse venue at 5.30 pm sharp in order to be ready in time for the 7 pm soft opening for GENY INUSRANCE.

I understand some of you thought that it would be unnecessary to pay them for the hour and half it takes to set up, but I also remember that happening with the last event, and in turn having to explain to the client why there were no bathroom facilities available.

My supervisor Clara couldn't find the company card at the time of booking, so I've had to put down deposits on my debit account. Is there someone I can talk to about how I can get paid back for this?

All in all, the entertainment and decorations are all organised and I hope to see some of you there. Very exciting.

Cheers,

Jessica

While some members of staff seemed relieved that every single errand had been accounted for by the meaningless intern, language used in the email seemed to rub some of her superiors the wrong way.

CFO Rosie Alcott says she had no idea who Jessica was until she read that email, which had been forwarded to her by someone who was claiming to have completed all of those tasks himself.

'Cheers?' she says condescendingly. 'Is that what it's come to? We aren't working for the Red Cross. She may as well have finished with "hooroo". What was her name again?'

At time of press, Jessica was seen alone in a freezing-cold garage organising pull-up banners for the event that no one will be going to because it's a soft opening for an insurance company.

Steve Price Provides 'Well-Informed Opinion' On Whatever He Thinks Will Fire Up The Boomers

PROMINENT TALKBACK PERSONALITY and completely unaccomplished post-war Australian Steve Price has appeared on a popular TV panel show tonight to provide balance to an otherwise mutually agreed upon topic of common sense.

And by balance, they mean a well-informed opinion that is based around saying exactly the opposite of what the women and brown man are saying, in the hope of bringing about an emotive response from the like-minded semi-retired silver-haired undervalued

Australian men sitting at home who are longing for a sense of victimhood after a lifetime of right-place-right-time privilege and wealth-hoarding.

'No, that's absolute rubbish,' says Steve Price, regarding a specific societal issue that looks like it might require a slight compromise from middle-class Caucasian baby boomers.

After being met with several convincing arguments that conflict with his hot-button-pressing opinion, Steve Price is quick to either claim that he is being bullied for having

a baseless opinion, or that everyone else is carrying a sense of unwarranted entitlement for even suggesting that he could possibly imagine himself in someone else's shoes.

When the argument inevitably reaches the point of discussing a quite possible life-or-death hypothetical, the professional social commentator makes it clear that he doesn't care if anyone, or anything, dies in order to maintain his base level of first-world comfort.

Confused Boomer Having Trouble With Flip Phone Seeks Help From Equally Confused Gen Z

'FUCK!' HE SHOUTED. 'Nathan! Get out here!'

A local 13-year-old felt his stomach drop.

Had his father finally cottoned on to the fact his garden hose was getting progressively shorter? Did Dad open an email from his English teacher explaining that the recent detention he got was for pretending his glue stick was a penis?

As young Nathan Washbrook walked the long walk from the living room to the verandah, all these questions and more were racing through his head.

But a wave of relief washed over him, like a fully clothed tourist stuck in a rip and pulled out of the water by a Bondi Rescue lifeguard as soon as he got outside.

'How do you drive this fucking wookatook piece of shit?' yelled George Washbrook, a perennially angry and frustrated local baby boomer who has by the grace of God somehow avoided a serious cardiac episode thus far in his life. 'I was trying to send a message to your sister and it fucking disappeared.'

He was huffing and shaking at this point.

However, in a cruel twist of fate, Nathan looked at the half-fucked Motorola Razr and shrugged.

'I don't know how to use those things either, Dad,' he said. 'Let me take a look, but.'

After a few minutes of dicking about, Nathan was able to find his way back to the message his father was attempting to compose.

Confiding in our reporter, Nathan said the message was not to his sister but to George's receptionist.

'Why do bad things happen to good people?' he asked *The Advocate* while our reporter was buying him cigarettes at Sully's Newsagency in South Betoota.

Our reporter shrugged – he didn't know – but assured the Year 7 student at the Whooton Academy that what goes around, ultimately comes around.

More to come.

Font Size On Boomer's iPhone Visible From Across The Room

AN AGEING HOME OWNER was the talk of the Royal Betoota Yacht Squadron today after fellow home owners began mocking the 66-year-old over the size of the font on his iPhone.

Dudley Raleigh, a semi-retired piano tuner from Betoota Grove, was left red-faced this afternoon as the contents of his messages were able to be seen from the other side of the marina by younger, equally well-heeled members.

Our reporter was present on the scene as the oddly wealthy man bore the brunt of the ageist bullying.

'Look at that,' laughed one 21-year-old Chris-Craft enthusiast. 'I can read his messages from here [laughs]! How about you book yourself a visit to OPSM or something? How's your macula? I can tell it's fucked from here!'

A short but polite chorus of laughter erupted from the friends of the 24-foot launch owner, who even had the gall to point.

Mr Raleigh, however, saw the lighter side of the conversation as he waved at the youths. Speaking – in hindsight, unnecessarily – to *The Advocate* about the confrontation, Raleigh said he didn't mind the banter.

'When I was a young fulla, we used to take the mickey out of old codgers all the time. Like I guess I am now,' he said. 'We had this one maths teacher who had these two huge hearing aids basically bolted onto the sides of his head. We used to call him Mr Radar! Anyway, one day Radar comes into class and we all speak very softly to him on purpose. So he turns his hearing aids up to the max, thinking he just had them too low. Then we all screamed at the top of our lungs and old Radar's head almost blew up! Piss funny. Anyway, nice talking to you. I have to go wash the Riviera down now.'

More to come.

Study Confirms Gen X Are Just Boomers Who Like *Star Wars*

A RECENT STUDY conducted by Australia's peak scientific body, the CSIRO, has concluded and confirmed that Generation X are nothing but junior boomers who like *Star Wars*.

Speaking this morning to a handful of journalists outside the organisation's headquarters in Canberra, spokesman Larry Bernk said the findings weren't that surprising and were largely expected.

'Most people don't really care about gen X,' he said. 'Which is something I personally find to ring true. When I open my mouth at work, the older guys roll their eyes at me just like the kid grads we have. We've actually got it hardest out of any generation. So when the findings of this study came in, I went into the staffroom to lambaste my colleagues for treating me like I was a member of the Silent Generation!

'They just told me to get fucked.'

However, Larry went on to explain that the one common thread among his generation is that they all enjoyed the original *Star Wars* movies more than the prequels.

'The new Disney ones are even worse!'

Our reporter clicked off his recorder and told Larry to get fucked.

More to come.

> *Our reporter clicked off his recorder and told Larry to get fucked. More to come.*

Gen X Graphic Designer Renovates Terrace House Carport For His Prized Saab

GILLION ANDERSEN has finally shaken his builder's hand today and put the cherry on top of his new reno.

The 52-year-old father of two smiled at his builder's handiwork after the new carport he wanted to protect one of his most prized assets reached completion today.

The graphic designer from Betoota's French Quarter decided to undertake the 'stressful' and 'onerous' task of redoing his carport as a treat to his beloved Saab.

'I love her,' he laughed, motioning to the 2000 model car. 'I also love my wife,' he chortled, flicking some European-brand cigarette onto his driveway.

Like many gen Xers around the country, Andersen explained that the Saab brand has always had a special place in his heart.

'They are beautiful in their own right. An "anti-brand" brand,' he explained. 'The Swedish automobile perfectly says fuck conformity, and fuck the system that has benefited us so well, you know. So that's why I needed to protect my baby,' he said, referring to the car with an inexplicably placed ignition and an engine that would be better suited to a motorised scooter.

'Lord knows what I'll do if I have to get another car,' he said, referring to the fact that Saab has been defunct for a few years now.

Andersen then told *The Advocate* that he isn't like every other gen Xer who loves the 'left of centre brand'.

'Did you see the way my name was a spelt?' he said. 'Not your typical "Anderson". I mean, my family's been in the country for three generations, but there is a bit of Scandi blood running through my veins.

'Geez, they've got it right over there,' he added, before launching into a lecture about the ways in which Scandinavian countries are miles ahead of us.

Our reporter left at that point.

Millennials Begin Poking Needles Into Vacant Investment Properties To Drive Down House Prices

STRUGGLING FIRST HOME BUYERS may have found an easy foot into the hyper-inflated Australian property market, it has been confirmed.

Mirroring the damage done to Australian fruit growers over the last fortnight, local millennial Courtney Fisher (25) has starting randomly poking needles into the plasterboard walls of investment properties in her childhood suburb.

'It's the only way,' she says. 'The negative gearing tax has allowed houses to sit vacant for no reason. It's pretty much just land-banking, one out of three houses in my parents'

street are empty . . . So I've started putting needles in them [mwahaha],' she laughed.

'I thought, if a bunch of needles can cripple a market with an actually sustainable level of supply and demand, I should at least give it a crack on one that is manipulated against me.'

Courtney is just one of hundreds of thousands of Australians who are currently locked out of the Australian housing market, despite having at least triple the savings her parents did at her age when they were buying houses – on the same wages.

It seems a vast number of fellow first home buyers have had a similar

idea, with reports that almost half the houses in Australian capital cities were unable to sell over the weekend due to reports of needle contamination.

'We are worried about the effects this will have on the market,' said *Domain* magazine editor Wyatt Oldguy (66).

'At worst, this will encourage home owners to sell to the first bidder, instead of waiting to sell it to some foreign investor sight unseen.'

Inner City Local Boomers Need TV Volume On 60 But Can Still Hear Wine Bar Two Blocks Over

A PAIR OF SOCIAL, ECONOMIC AND POLITICAL HANDBRAKES on our progressive desert community have told *The Advocate* this morning that while they need their television volume to be nearly at the max, they can still hear a popular wine bar two blocks over at night-time.

New French Quarter empty-nesters, Dale and Mango Pearson, moved into the cultural heart of our town from Betoota Heights halfway through last year and they've loved their new home thus far.

Speaking this morning to our reporter at the Pisse Dans Ma Poche Bistro on the fabled Champs de Tuer Tous Les Anciens, the sexagenarians say their peaceful existence is often disturbed by noisy drunks, rooftop bars and amplified music.

'We love it here in the French Quarter,' said Dale. 'There's so much to do, as well as the culture and the pretty buildings. Now that the kids have moved out, we can get on with the business of spending the kids' inheritance [laughs].'

But not all is well, as Mango describes.

'There's a lot of loud bars here that are really taking the mickey when it comes to being part of the fabric of the French Quarter,' she said.

'We can hear this one bar that has French folk music every Saturday night. It's two blocks from here and we can still hear it! I feel like driving my car into it and then telling the police I just had a "senior moment". They wouldn't send me to jail, a little old lady!'

All this despite the couple's penchant for having their television turned up to an antisocial level.

Our reporter spoke to a few of the boomer fucks' neighbours in the new Beriton apartment development on the corner of Rue de Putain and Branlette.

One neighbour, who asked to remain anonymous, said that they're often disturbed by Mango and Dale's television volume but are too afraid to speak up about it.

'Some nights, I lie in bed while I hear *Grand Designs* blaring in the next room through the paper-thin Beriton walls and I just hope to God one of their ventricles blows out and I get some peace,' they said.

'It's so loud and I'm so tired. But they own the flat and I just rent with three friends, so I don't have any power here. Only God can help us now.'

More to come.

Confused Boomer Attempts To Move Against The Flow Of Passengers Disembarking Plane

A GIBBERING OLD FUCK was seen attempting to move against the flow of disembarking passengers today shortly after the 3.20 pm Qantas service to town landed.

While some immediately and needlessly stood as the plane pulled up at the ramp, Graeme Ponk was determined to be different.

The 68-year-old didn't remain seated, he didn't try to stand up in the race to be first off the plane. He did something much, much more unique.

Speaking exclusively to *The Advocate* this afternoon, fellow passenger Emily Spearman detailed what the confused, terrified baby boomer did next.

'This old bloke started walked towards the back of the plane, even though there weren't any back steps,' she said. 'He was moaning about being unable to find his bag or something. It was in the overhead bins opposite his seat. We could all see it. Fuck me dead, don't ever let me get that old and afraid. Come to my house on my 60th birthday and shoot me through the brain like at the end of *The Departed* or something. That looks like hell. You could see everyone on the plane looking at Graeme with absolute disgust.'

Mercifully, an errant steward appeared to corral the intrepid sexagenarian into going back with the flow. He helped Graeme find his carry-on luggage and told him on which carousel to find his checked bags – to which Graeme asked:

'What on Earth is a carousel, and why does it have my bags!'

More to come.

The 68-year-old didn't remain seated, he didn't try to stand up in the race to be first off the plane. He did something much, much more unique.

Boomers Visit Great Barrier Reef One Last Time Before Their Generation Finally Kills It

'WE DIDN'T KNOW we were killing the planet,' they said.

'So it's not our fault. Believe us, we feel really bad about what we've done to Earth but in reality, it's not really our problem, is it?'

Graham and Butter Rogers, an ageing Betoota Grove couple, have recently returned home to our cosmopolitan desert community after a short holiday to the Great Barrier Reef.

They both wanted to see the globe's largest living organism one last time before their generation, the most spoilt in human history, finally kills it.

'The last time we went was in 1995, with our young family,' said Butter, a lifelong homemaker and Rotary Club member.

'I just remember all the fish and coral. It was beautiful. I know it's sad to say but Graham and I don't have much longer and we wanted to see the reef one last time before it dies. Which will obviously be way before us.'

Graham said the reef looked much different from the one he saw in the mid-1990s and that made him feel guilty.

He explained to *The Advocate* that

while he fells somewhat guilty on behalf of his generation for the 'disgusting' and 'embarrassing' impact their petulant sense of self-worth has had on the environment, he is also glad that death is coming soon for him.

'I can't imagine what this planet will look like when my grandson is my age,' he said. 'He'll probably end up being bayoneted by a Russian teenager in some Turkmenistan oilfield during a conflict over oil, water or food. And to some extent, my generation will be responsible. Oh well.'

More to come.

Labor Folds And Announces Boomers Can Trade Franking Credits For Pieces Of Bleached Coral

FEDERAL LABOR has proven once again that they're simply the diet version of the Coalition this morning by announcing that boomer fucks can trade their franking credits for bits of Great Barrier Reef coral their entitled generation has bleached beyond recognition.

This is the second capitulation Bill Shorten, known locally in the Diamantina as the de-Jesus-ed ScoMo, has let happen in the past 48 hours.

The first being his idle bipartisanship in letting Nauru and Manus medical evacuations be diverted to Christmas Island first.

However, in this latest backflip, Labor said today that while they can't simply give an entitled boomer money for nothing, they can meet them in the middle.

Speaking to journalists today, Shorten explained that his party is in the business of winning an election, not making progressive inner city elites feel warm and fuzzy inside like the Greens.

'We understand that boomers are entitled to live a long and happy life in retirement,' said Shorten. 'Even if that means somebody else has to pay for it. But while we cannot afford to give people with enormous share portfolios money for simply being that wealthy, we can give them another token of appreciation: pieces of bleached coral.'

The Advocate reached out to the Coalition for comment but have yet to receive a reply.

Local Boomer Races Back Into Burning Home To Save The Franking Credits

PUSHING HIS WAY through firefighters late last night, a local baby boomer threw caution to the wind and raced back into his burning Betoota Grove home to save his franking credits from certain destruction.

Roger Allen-Cole, the 71-year-old hero, survived the ordeal, but tragically, his franking credits did not.

At approximately 11 pm last night, a fire broke out at the Allen-Cole residence on Whiteshoe Crescent, with local firefighting crews arriving on the scene shortly after.

All occupants of the house managed to make it out before the blaze took hold, however, Roger says his most valuable possession was still inside.

Speaking to our reporters this morning in front of the smouldering ashes of his family home, Mr Allen-Cole said he was ultimately glad his wife, son and two granddaughters made it out unharmed, but he's not sure how he's going to go without his beloved franking credits.

'I don't know what I'm going to do now. I feel lost,' he said. 'Without that cash injection each year, I might be forced into making changes to my lifestyle that I shouldn't have to. I've paid my fair share in tax, I've been lucky in business. Why punish me and other people cut from the same cloth as I?

'My franking credits are more important to me than anything else. More than the environment I'm leaving for my grandchildren. More than health care for people less wealthy than me. More than state education. If it wasn't for our home and contents insurance, I'd be ruined.'

The Nine Network Imparja news team pulled up to the scene and Mr Allen-Cole excused himself from our reporter.

'Sorry, Errol. The news cameras are here and I need to make myself cry before they turn them on.'

Our reporter nodded and patted the economic and social anchor on the back as he rubbed his eyes furiously.

More to come.

'Without that cash injection each year, I might be forced into making changes to my lifestyle that I shouldn't have to.'

Young Voter Looks Forward To Ruining Boomers' Financial Future Like They Ruined The Environment

A YOUNG VOTER WITH VERY CONTROVERSIAL OPINIONS told *The Advocate* this morning that she's looking forward to getting back at our town's baby boomers the only way she can – at the polls.

In particular, their franking credits, which Labor vows to remove once they get into power.

That would leave a number of self-funded retirees in the wider Diamantina Basin out of pocket, putting added stress on Lake Betoota's stalling motor yacht and sailing boat trade.

But Gracie Stevenson (19) says she doesn't care.

'Boo hoo,' she mimed to our reporter. 'You get money, you pay tax. Simple as that. No free lunches, I couldn't give a brass fuck if you've worked your whole life. If I had my way, we'd put people to sleep at 64 when they start becoming a drain on the economy. I've got no qualms about being dragged out of bed at midnight on my 64th birthday and switched off permanently with a pneumatic bolt if it's for the greater good. I'm just sick of their entitlement. I'm looking forward to ruining the financial future of the boomers in this shithole on the edge of the Simpson Desert just the same as the boomers destroyed the planet for everyone.'

The Advocate reached out to some local baby boomers for comment on Ms Stevenson's offensive 'Kill All Boomers' sign and opinions on them in general, and all were ready to throw in their two cents.

Graham Smith of Betoota Grove said young people don't understand that not all boomers are rich. Many boomers are, in fact, hard done by.

'Not all boomers,' said the 69-year-old. 'Not all boomers buy yachts and convertibles with their franking credits. Others, like me, use their franking credits to give our children a leg up in the property market with a deposit. Some pay their grandchildren's private school fees. Useful things like protecting their wealth and safeguarding it for their family's future. I'd rather paint the roof Cobain-style than see my great grandchildren at East Betoota Central High.'

The rest of the opinions were basically verbatim to that of Mr Smith's so in the interest of saving newspaper inches, ink and the environment, *The Advocate*'s editors decided to omit them.

More to come.

> *'I couldn't give a brass fuck if you've worked your whole life. If I had my way, we'd put people to sleep at 64 when they start becoming a drain on the economy.'*

Local Upper-Middle-Class Mother Confuses 'Cool Mum' Title With Criminal Negligence

A BETOOTA GROVE MOTHER OF THREE told reporters this morning that she's a 'cool mum' – just hours before police arrested her at the six-bedroom Tudor revival home on Whiteshoe Crescent.

Bernice Cole Watson, 46, has been charged by police for supplying alcohol to her youngest child who was due to attend a small gathering of friends this evening in the local area.

Authorities were tipped off by a bottle shop attendant who alleges that Mrs Watson, a mid-level marketing 'double diamond' sales executive, told the man that she was buying the alcohol for her underage daughter because she was a 'cool mum'.

Prior to her arrest this afternoon, Mrs Watson boldly bragged about her crimes to our reporter, who'd just enjoyed a cone in his wife's Tarago during the lunch break in the car park of the Old City District Vintage Cellars which sits opposite *The Advocate*'s Daroo Street newsroom.

'My mother used to buy me alcohol,' she said, talking at our reporter through the driver's side window. 'She was a cool mum. She used to go off with her friends and leave the house to me and my friends and we'd have boys over and everything!'

Our reporter looked down into the centre console of the Tarago to see if he'd accidentally taken a hit out of the changa bag instead of the weed because this unwarranted admission of criminal negligence by Mrs Watson to a stranger came across as weird.

Noticing our reporter was barely keeping it together, Mrs Watson closed the rear hatch of her late-model GLA Mercedes and left.

More to come.

Gen X Leftie Brought To Orgasm During Mid-Afternoon Paul Keating YouTube Session

A LOCAL VOLVO AND SEX PISTOLS ENTHUSIAST has today had to run to the bathroom in a hurry.

The scurry out of the open-plan marketing agency came after the gen X leftie decided to treat himself to a spontaneous mid-afternoon Paul Keating YouTube session.

Aldous Peters spoke to *The Advocate* a short time ago after he'd successfully managed to flush his underwear down the toilet following a five-minute shift trying to dispose of the sullied garment.

'Geez, I won't be doing that again in public,' said the free-balling self-described free spirit as he washed his hands.

'I thought I'd treat some of the millennials in our office to some real political discourse,' said the man who affectionately refers to the former PM as PJK. 'And I got the blood rush when he referred to John Howard as a little desiccated coconut. Then unfortunately mid-way through the line about debating John Hewson being equivalent to getting flogged with wet lettuce, I nutted.'

Shaking his head and splashing his face with water, Peters then told us he hopes he doesn't get a talking to from HR.

'I should have walked away, but that razor-sharp wit, that intellect, that charisma, I'm just a deer in the headlights.'

'I got the blood rush when he referred to John Howard as a little desiccated coconut.'

Boomers Celebrate Election Victory By Treating Themselves To A Fresh Pair Of Merrells

THE GRADE ONE HIKING TRAILS around town are quivering in fear this afternoon as a breeding pair of local baby boomers have celebrated the Coalition election victory by treating themselves to fresh pair of Merrell boots – each.

Greg and Bucket Heimans were losing sleep earlier this month because the prospect of Bill Shorten and his troupe of inner city Bjelke-Petersen apologists winning the election would've meant their plans for retirement probably would've had to change.

However, now that Bill has been thrown into the same annals of history as Simon Crean, Mark Lathan and Kim Beazley, the 70-year-olds can rest easy once again.

Speaking to *The Advocate* this afternoon while they sat in the boot of their late-model Land Rover Discovery lacing up their new Merrells, the Gemini and Leo laughed as they described the sense of relief they felt last Saturday night.

'My oh my,' said Greg, a semi-retired author. 'I thought we were going to have to go back to work!'

Bucket, too, was pleased her nest egg is finally safe from the asylum seekers and the big government that defends their rights to commit acts of terror once they arrive here in Australia.

However, she's not content with just a new pair of hiking boots.

'I'm looking at the new 2020 Subaru Outback,' she said. 'It's not like I need a new car, it's just that now Scott is back in charge, I can afford some luxuries. I've worked hard my whole life and I think I deserve to treat myself. The Liberals understand that, which is why I voted for the Liberal Democrats.

'Are you going to join us on the hike?'

Our reporter indicated that he would not.

More to come.

Tesla Engineers Baffled As Local Boomer Manages To Install 44 Viruses Into Car's Computer

A LOCAL BABY BOOMER, who thought purchasing an overpriced luxury electric vehicle would absolve him of all guilt for his generation's role in signing the planet's death warrant, has somehow managed to install over 40 malicious viruses into his Tesla's on-board computer – leaving engineers at the US car maker 'baffled'.

Graham Walters, who made his money exploiting loopholes in our nation's regressive tax system that rewards dishonesty and punishes the poor, told the Tesla boffins that he didn't know how the viruses got inside his car.

The 69-year-old said the same thing to our reporter this afternoon.

'My grandson plays games on it sometimes,' he said. 'That must be it. I told his mother not to let him play in my nice new car! Damn it!'

However, some of the Tesla robots that are currently masquerading as human beings said that they've narrowed it down to a few avenues of investigation.

Speaking exclusively to *The Advocate* this afternoon via the floating pieces of celestial human faeces this government often refers to as the Sky Muster NBN, Peter Caper from Tesla said some of the things they uncovered in Mr Washbrook's car have 'really rattled' his team.

'I'm not sure if I should be telling you this, you know?' he said. 'But that old guy who owns the car with the viruses in it, he's been looking at some of the most depraved pornography I've ever seen. On his car computer, while he's been driving around. Like it's full-on scat porn. I had to take a day off work after I saw it.

'The telemetry and tracking information suggests he drives around with it playing on the big screen, then sometimes he pulls over to shave the carrot on the side of the road. None us knows what to do. We aren't able to deal with this, so we just did a format and handed it back to him.

'Don't tell anybody I told you this. I don't know how he's managed to install 44 computer viruses into a car but anything is possible when a boomer is left unsupervised with technology.'

More to come.

MINOR
GRIEVANCES

Thanks to the selfish nature of politics, the carnival-like atmosphere of the Federal Senate is likely to grow progressively more stale as time marches on. Thanks to preference whispering and the collating of votes, minor parties found themselves in the spotlight after each election. Now that the rules have changed, the glory days of having grossly under-qualified lawmakers in this country are over.

But what makes a person qualified to make laws? From Senator Ricky Muir of the Motoring Enthusiasts Party to Senator Glenn Lazarus of Clive and later on, himself – these are the Australians who, we at *The Advocate,* feel were the most qualified people to make law in the country because they were Australians. They'd tried, they'd failed. They'd tried, they'd succeeded.

They added personality and zest to the least interesting cog in the Westminster system's gearbox.

But they're gone.

Not all of them, however.

The matriarch of the Independents Jacqui Lambie is back. So you can rest assured the political classes of Sydney Uni Old Boys and Canberra-bubble-lifers will be held accountable for any policies that are likely to make life any harder than it already is in the housos.

Unfortunately, joining Lambie is the most malignant handbrake on social and economic progress in Australia as well, Pauline Hanson.

The sophomoric and unfunny Derryn Hinch is gone, off Sky News to upset people. One thing to remember with Derryn is that it's only his beard that makes him look powerful. Without it, he looks as threatening as Aunty Sue's new boyfriend attending his first family Christmas.

Avid rower Cory Bernardi is back again and like Olympic rowers do, he's going backwards in a hurry.

Two other South Australians from the Centre Alliance are also joining Cory in the red room, which makes you wonder what in Christ's name is going on in South Australia? Rounded vowels, hip hop, flavoured milk and alternative batteries. Weird.

Some Greens are in the Senate this time, hopefully they can put aside their factional problems long enough to do something for the environment. Here's hoping. They're probably the last chance the ecosystem has in seeing the start of the next century. Good luck to them.

For how different they are, the halcyon days of the Senate might be over but the upper house will continue to be the most fun to be in.

Clive Palmer Listed As 2017 Archibald Finalist With Breathtaking Self-Portrait

RETIRED POLITICIAN and Queensland mining icon Clive Palmer has blown away the insular Australian art community today, after being listed as an Archibald finalist with a moving and heartbreakingly honest self-portrait.

Titled *Clive* (100 cm x 50 cm), the oil painting has offered a rare insight into the embattled businessman's current state of mind, in a world of boat cruises, court cases and high-quality memes.

'This is me. This is the most honest look you will get at me. Forget the fake news. Forget Murdoch. This is the real Clive.'

The 63-year-old mineral magnate and former leader of the Palmer United Party is paying odds of $0.50 to take out the iconic winner's sash, according to the TAB.

Director of the Art Gallery of NSW, Nolan Hart, says it's good to include a few high-profile non-artists to really get things going.

'Clive was one of those dark horses that we rarely get to see in this industry dominated by art-school-educated practising artists. We have made a concerted effort to include a few one-hit wonders, or other equally novel finalists – it's a great way of creating a bit of buzz. The Edgecliff Boys' Grammar portrait of their retiring headmaster, for example, offers a rare portal into the life and achievements of Caucasian white men that live five kilometres away from our gallery.'

In its 96th year, the Archibald Prize is touted as one of the most prestigious art prizes in the country – with approximately 800 entrants each year submitting portraits-of-photographs of B-list Australian actors, other artists, and moderately well-known ex-politicians.

The Art Gallery of NSW announced this morning the 43 finalists in the running for the Archibald Prize. Some of the artists with strong works in contention include Brisbane graffiti artist SOFLES, who has painted fellow artist Ben Quilty, Anh Do's portrait of himself; Nicholas Harding's portrait of John Olsen and Melbourne rapper 360 with his stunning portrait of ABC *Q&A* host Tony Jones.

Lambie Says High Court Decision May Take Her Job But It Will Never Take Her Freedom

AS THE AUSTRALIAN FEDERAL GOVERNMENT faces its most dramatic constitutional crisis since we somehow managed to lose a sitting Prime Minister at sea, whispers are bouncing around the halls of Parliament House as public servants who would never be able to find a six-figure salary in any other job desperately dob each other in for having wog parents.

Another senator now looks like falling victim to the ongoing citizenship crisis within 24 hours, with Tasmanian Independent Jacqui Lambie awaiting urgent advice from British authorities as to whether she is a dual citizen.

This means there is a possibility of a complete stranger with absolutely zero experience as a politician stepping in to replace Lambie in the Australian upper house.

Senator Lambie has said she sought urgent advice last week as to whether she holds dual citizenship, and that she will resign from the Senate immediately if that is confirmed.

Speaking to *The Betoota Advocate* this afternoon, Senator Lambie was more than nonplussed about this particular issue.

'Oh for fuck's sake,' she roared. 'How the fuck was I supposed to know?'

As Lambie's recently acknowledged Scottish blood boils, she stormed from her office in full Mel Gibson face paint.

'You know what, I'm sick of all of these High Court toffs taking Aussie jobs from hard-working Aussie politicians.'

The iconic Tasmanian offered some words of advice to her fellow pollies facing the same issues.

'Aye,' she yelled in a broad Tasmanian accent. 'Fight and you may get the sack. Run and you'll get a job on the board of a massive corporation – at least for a while. And dying in your beds many years from now, would you be willing to trade all the days from this day to that for one chance to sit on $200K a year to abuse people in the Senate?

'Just one chance to come back here and tell the High Court that they may take our jobs but they'll never take our freedom!'

> *As Lambie's recently acknowledged Scottish blood boils, she stormed from her office in full Mel Gibson face paint. 'You know what, I'm sick of all of these High Court toffs taking Aussie jobs from hard-working Aussie politicians.'*

Katter Welcomes Banking Royal Commission But He Ain't Spending Any More Time On It Because, In The Meantime, Every Three Months, A Person Is Torn To Pieces By A Crocodile In North Queensland

MAVERICK NORTH QUEENSLAND MP the Honourable Bob Katter III has today commended the Turnbull Government for 'growing a set' and announcing a royal commission into the banking sector, after Australia's big four banks wrote to the Treasurer asking for an inquiry to restore public faith in the financial system.

Turnbull fronted media today alongside Scott Morrison MP to declare that he will be receiving a lot fewer Christmas cards this year.

'Since the financial crisis, there have been examples of misconduct by financial institutions. Some of them extremely serious. And that's demanded a response from the institutions themselves and from government,' said Mr Turnbull.

'ANZ, Commonwealth, NAB and Westpac – all eyes on you, motherfuckers. Those who need to get got, will get got.'

However, Katter, who has been one of the most vocal supporters of a banking royal commission, has already turned his attention to the next biggest issue facing his electorate.

'Our farmers have had their backs to the wall as a result of stand-over tactics from these bastards in Martin Place,' he said. 'It's about bloody time. I commend Turnbull and his cronies for making this decision – may a thousand banking executives go to prison – but I ain't spending any more time on it, because in the meantime, every three months, a person is torn to pieces by a crocodile in north Queensland.'

Turnbull is yet to comment on whether or not he would entertain a royal commission into why every three months a person is torn to pieces by a crocodile in north Queensland.

Bob Katter Refuses To Disclose Where His Deadly New Boots Came From

THE HONOURABLE BOB KATTER III MP has told journalists he won't be spending any more time on the issue that surrounds where he got his flash new boots.

The leather boots, which don't look like they've been made by his mates at Prospect Street, appear to be made out of a reptilian animal hide.

This has led to questions about whether Katter may have been discreetly killing crocodiles in the Deep North, following his blow-up about civilian deaths related to the animal late last year.

In a doorstop interview following the marriage equality plebiscite result, Mr Katter said people were 'entitled to their sexual proclivities, let there be a thousand blossoms bloom' before his demeanour darkened and he declared he would spend no more time on the topic.

'Because in the meantime, every three months a person is torn to pieces by a crocodile in north Queensland,' he said.

In response to accusations that he has been firing bullets into the now endangered lounge lizards, Katter was quick to put his dukes up.

'A mate gave 'em to me. Why do you care?' roared the maverick north Queensland Independent after being met with a media scrum on his way out of Parliament House.

'Sorry, should I be wearing square-toed Italian leather when I grace the halls of Parliament House? That's not what we do in the Curry. Maybe in Point Piper – but not up top. The leather is red. Have a look at it. It's as red as Di Natale. Crocs aren't red. Don't even pretend you delusional southerners know what a croc looks like.

'I'm not spending any more time on it.'

In a doorstop interview following the marriage equality plebiscite result, Mr Katter said people were 'entitled to their sexual proclivities, let there be a thousand blossoms bloom' before his demeanour darkened and he declared he would spend no more time on the topic.

ABC Fact Checker Explodes After Being Tasked With Checking Everything Bob Katter Said Today About Anning

A SUPERCOMPUTER at the heart of the ABC's Fact-Checking Unit has reportedly exploded this afternoon after a staff member gave it the task of fact-checking each part of Bob Katter's press conference today.

Around lunchtime today (AEST) Katter spoke to the media in Cairns, despite it being a sitting day for both houses in Canberra, where he made a number of claims about everything from the foundation of the city of Cairns to his own personal heritage and the nation's immigration policy.

Over the course of roughly 20 minutes, the Member for Kennedy allegedly made upwards of 400 claims that needed to be verified.

About an hour after Katter was done talking, a taxpayer-funded employee of the public broadcaster finished typing the speech into the fact-checking computer and pressed 'enter'.

'That's when the fire alarm went off,' said the head of ABC's Fact-Checking Unit, Harriet Fuller.

Ms Fuller spoke to *The Advocate* via public telephone a short time ago.

'The whole building shook violently. My green tea spilled all over my desk. I looked around at my co-workers and we all traded worried looks. Then the office started to fill with smoke and the fire warden came in and told us all to get the hell out.

'I believe the supercomputer exploded after one of my staff asked it to fact-check everything Bob Katter said today. They really should've broken it up into smaller bits. I don't know much more, I'll get back to you later.'

From what witnesses have been able to describe, a large hole was blown out of the north side of the ABC Kremlin in Ultimo, in the heart of Sydney's soulless district.

Emergency crews are currently attending the scene with no reports of casualties at the time of print.

Greens Hipster All For #MeToo Movement Except When It Involves White-Ant Subordinate Females

WITH THE RESIGNATION of a NSW Labor leader, and whispers surrounding a number of other left-wing politicians, ▮▮▮▮▮▮▮▮▮▮ ▮▮▮▮▮▮▮▮▮▮▮▮▮▮ the nation's inner city elite are now on par with AFL fans as Australia's most staunch apologists for sexual harassment.

In fact, so engrained is the culture of sexual entitlement and hipster chauvinism within Australia's inner city progressive circles, Victorian Greens may lose up to five seats in the state's upper house – following several months of #MeToo accusations made against prominent state and federal politicians, campaigners and candidates.

After the party was rocked with internal accusations surrounding both assaults and the subsequent protection of, or indifference towards, alleged perpetrators, thousands of young privileged white hipsters are distraught that they can no longer claim moral absolution.

'Don't get me wrong. I am 100 per cent a feminist,' says Richie Mund (27), a well-known vocal campaigner and son of two career public servants in high-paid and secure bureaucratic positions within either the ABC or the state library.

'But there's got to be a point when, you know, people are just using the #MeToo movement to stop us from achieving our end goal. Which is to force the Australian public to have frustrating and poorly articulated debates about gender theory in primary schools. Not to mention all the data we've been gathering on how kangaroos are nearly extinct.'

Richie says that while the #MeToo movement is very important for holding AFL stars and B-list actors accountable for their treatment of women, he never thought it would get to the point where he was unable to talk over people at dinner parties.

'Like, I know plenty of examples where the accusations aren't true and are just being used by unpaid volunteers to bring down certain politicians within our party that they have given so much time and energy to see succeed.'

Richie has no doubt that some of the lesser-ranked females, whose names he didn't know until they inconveniently accused high-profile Greens identities of sexual harassment, have a sinister agenda.

'Who knows what they are up to. It can't just be about wanting to air out the traumatic experiences they've suffered at the hands of these guys,' he says.

Katter Family Arrive Heavily Armed At Queensland Parliament House To Discuss Daylight Savings

THE HONOURABLE BOB KATTER III MP has today arrived in Brisbane with his son, Mount Isa state member Robbie Katter, to hold 'passionate talks' with the southern cowards that want to fiddle with the clocks.

This comes after an exclusive poll by *The Courier-Mail* revealed that 55 per cent of Queenslanders back a transition to daylight savings, while 41 per cent opposed it and 4 per cent were undecided.

The Katter family, who represent one of the most powerful political dynasties in north Queensland, have made it very clear over the past three decades that they sit squarely in the 41 per cent who oppose these changes.

'First you take all of our taxes to build a light rail project on the bloody Gold Coast, now you want us waking up in the dark,' spat a furious Bob Katter, who has indicated that he and his constituents are willing to spill blood over this issue.

'Either we succeed and stay in the same time zone, or you can load up your pissy little police-issue handguns and fight us.'

The new poll suggested that two-thirds of people living in the south-east want to see the changes introduced across Queensland. If the changes were to be implemented, clocks will be moved forward an hour in October and back an hour in April – like they do in the elitist southern states that Premier Annastacia Palaszczuk wishes we could be more like.

'We knew the bastards in Brisbane were planning something, and we knew this day would come,' said Robbie Katter. 'We have stockpiled our weapons and non-perishables; it's go-time. If you want it that way.'

Bob Katter MP reiterated his son's threats of a civil war.

'Give us AEST, UTC+10:00, or give us death!'

> *'Either we succeed and stay in the same time zone, or you can load up your pissy little police-issue handguns and fight us.'*

Pauline Scouts Outside Gates Of Wacol Prison Looking For Potential One Nation Candidates

ONE NATION LEADER Pauline Hanson has spent the day waiting outside Brisbane Correctional Centre looking for any paroled offenders who look like they have what it takes to run for One Nation.

'People get sent to this place from all over the state,' she says of the notorious supermax prison. 'So it's a good starting point to find people for all the different electorates that I haven't really touched on yet.'

This comes after Pauline Hanson says she will not disendorse a One Nation candidate after jokes about domestic violence were found on the Facebook page of his sex shop.

Mark Thornton, the candidate for Thuringowa, owns the Cupids Cabin Adult Shop in Townsville, which has a number of explicit posts on its Facebook page.

'It's just not that bad really,' Hanson says. 'Not as bad as the Asian bird I was gonna run down in Bundamba who said gays need electric shock therapy. And definitely not as bad as the bloke who kidnapped Aboriginal kids and mowed a swastika into his lawn while doing a Nazi salute.

'Probably should have vetted the social media accounts held by these guys a bit better though, hey.'

Environmentally Conscious Forklift Driver Dreams Of One Day Being Wealthy Enough To Vote Green

'IT'S SOMETHING I ASPIRE TO,' HE SAID.

'A brighter, more sustainable future for me and the planet. But first, I need to make some money.'

The road Mike Greenhauer is on is long.

It starts at the Betoota Ponds postal distribution depot and it finishes somewhere in the leafy cul-de-sacs of Betoota Grove.

The 26-year-old unionised forklift driver hopes that one day the biggest worry in his life will be the environment.

'Right now, it's job security and housing affordability that I'm most worried about,' he said. 'Then I guess it'd be wage growth and interest rates. But yeah, one day I'd like to be carefree enough to vote for the Greens.

'Rich enough, too.'

Mr Greenhauer understands that on his journey from the bottom to the top, he might even have to start voting Liberal when he becomes a small business–owning home owner and elects to manage his own super fund.

'It's part and parcel of growing up,' he said. 'Maybe I might even start worrying about immigration and people being disrespectful in general.'

Once his house is paid off, that is, and it's worth many hundreds of thousands more than what he bought it for – and he's essentially able to live off the franking credits his share portfolio is geared towards exploiting.

'But I will mellow in my middle age,' he conceded. 'The guilt of being who I am will end up crushing me. Like *The Tell-Tale Heart* beating under the floorboards of my renovated French Quarter terrace house! The shame and heartbreak of being successful will overwhelm me, I know. But it'll all wash away when I cast my vote for the Greens. Even though they're the most divided and toothless major party, I don't care. The environment is too important. I look forward to that day.'

Katter Staffer Wonders Why He Even Bothers Writing Notes On Bob's Hands Anymore

ONE OF BOB KATTER'S key policy advisors let out a heavy sigh this afternoon as the locally popular Queensland politician spoke to the media in Cairns regarding the comments made yesterday by his Senate leader, Fraser Anning.

Staffer Colin Overell sighed because once again, Bob didn't read any of the notes he had painstakingly written on the palm of each hand just moments before the press conference started.

He spoke to *The Advocate* in the minutes after the media scrum began to disperse.

'While we were still sitting in the Statesman, I wrote the notes on Bob's hands and I told him how the party stood on the issue,' said Overell. 'I said we must condemn Fraser and expel him from the party. There's simply too much at risk. Then I explained that an easy out of that line of questioning was to pull the old crocodile trick and get the country to meme about him harmlessly.

'But all that went out the window. His media advisor had their first cigarette in five years during that press conference. Honestly. But yeah, back to the notes. I don't even know why I bother doing it anymore. By the looks of things, he doesn't even read them – let alone take what I have to say on board. I'm not sure how we're going to get out of this one.'

Our reporter's conversation with Overell was abruptly interrupted by Katter himself, who allegedly snatched the phone away from his staffer to continue his tongue-lashing of the media.

'And another thing!' shouted Bob. 'Who am I speaking to here? I don't care! You're probably some black puffer vest–wearing, brown-boot brigade south-east corner bedwetter who doesn't know what in green Jesus is going on up here in north Queensland!'

Colin could be heard trying to wrestle the phone back off Bob.

'Bob!'

The following seconds were inaudible until somebody let out a blood-curdling yell.

'Australia not for sale! Australia not for sale!'

Colin let out another sigh and said he'd ring back after work.

More to come.

Clive Palmer Accidentally Sends Text Message Meant For His Media Advisor To Ten Million People

JUST A DAY after political candidate Clive Palmer flew to the Menindee Lakes to help clean up the environmental disaster that is the mass fish kill with a deep fryer and a couple bags of frozen chips, it appears the north Queensland mining magnate is back in the headlines.

This time for sending yet another unsolicited text.

This week alone we have seen Palmer texting campaign promises to millions of voters without their permission. Yesterday's text landed at 7.47 am and was ironically pledging to ban unsolicited texts.

When elected, United Australia Party will ban unsolicited political text messages which Labor & Liberal have allowed, it read.

Today's text, however, appears to have been not even ironic, and more of a mistake.

This text read:

Oi what was the name of that restaurant on the way to Canberra from Sydney that does the satay pasta.

Fuk that was good.

Palmer has since addressed today's text message, stating that it was meant for his media advisor, whose name is Evan.

'"Evan" sits just above "Every single Australian" in my phone's contact list,' says Clive. 'It was an easy mistake to make, and a costly one too. At six cents a text . . . Anyway, I apologise for the first one but not the other one. To be honest, I'm just getting really excited to get elected again and want to see if all my favourite haunts are still open. For the record, the restaurant's name is the Paragon Cafe in Goulburn. It's incredible.'

Greens Call For Immediate Ban On Floods After 300,000 Head Of Cattle Drown In The North-West

GREENS LEADER Richard Di Natale has fronted the media in Melbourne this morning calling for drastic action on flooding, and the cruel things that it does to animals.

Following the estimated deaths of 300,000 cattle in north-west Queensland, the Greens, in partnership with PETA, the RSPCA and that other animals rights organisation that has been leaking farmers' phone numbers, has today called for the urgent ban on floods across the country.

The Greens Party leader and senator from Victoria said he and his party members agreed that a total prohibition should be placed on weather events like a once-in-a-lifetime flood in the north-west region after they saw some pictures of dying cattle.

It is not yet known if *Four Corners* has cameras on the ground in Cloncurry – but one thing is for sure, the entire cattle industry will be made to suffer because of this one-off event that the cattle industry really had no part in.

With his knee springing forward sporadically during the press conference, Di Natale explained that the weather events should be banned in order to ensure that inner city residents aren't confronted with pictures detailing the harsh reality for many people living in rural and regional Australia.

'I don't even think we should be allowed water in these areas. Not at this rate. Not until my voter base has calmed down.'

The ALP has joined the Greens in their hysterical response to these emotive images and clarified that they too believe farmers are somehow responsible for this tragedy that they have been working tirelessly to avoid without proper dams and any other form of promised infrastructure.

There have even been reports of inner city Greens voters collapsing of thirst, after the images sparked a grassroots movement to boycott water.

Di Natale explained that the weather events should be banned in order to ensure that inner city residents aren't confronted with pictures detailing the harsh reality for many people living in rural and regional Australia.

WINNER WINNER **WINNER** WINNER **WINNER** WINNER **WINNER** WINNER **WINNER** WINNER **WINN**

$20,000

sunrise

QLD: KFC ONE-PUNCH ATTACKER CHARGED WITH MURDER   CAN 15°   8.39

Sunrise Producers Workshop Ideas To Repair One Nation's Tattered Image Ahead Of Election

PRODUCERS FROM the highest-rating breakfast television program in the country have put their minds together to come up with ways to repair One Nation's image before the federal election.

The party is reeling from an explosive Al Jazeera investigation that aired overnight that showed several prominent One Nation figures asking for large, foreign political donations from gun groups.

It comes after One Nation's de facto leader, Pauline Hanson, called for an end to foreign donations to political parties.

Network Seven's *Sunrise*, a program that prides itself in giving organisations such as One Nation a platform to spew hate speech and racist policy, say they're working around the clock to come up with ways to distract the populace from this latest incident.

One producer, who spoke briefly to *The Advocate* via phone, said one idea is to let Pauline be a 'Celebrity Cash Cow' for a week in the hope that presenting her in such a disarming circumstance will make her seem less of a bumbling racist to the voting public.

Another brainstorming session resulted in a remote segment with Mark Latham and David 'Kochie' Koch putting their differences aside and hosting a sausage sizzle in the foyer of The Australian Club.

At the time of press, the workshopping sessions were still under way.

More to come.

One idea is to let Pauline be a 'Celebrity Cash Cow' for a week in the hope that presenting her in such a disarming circumstance will make her seem less of a bumbling racist to the voting public.

Used Bus Condom Wins Local Preselection For Clive Palmer's United Australia Party

A POPULAR CONDOM found earlier this week inside out and stuck to a local bus has won preselection for Clive Palmer's controversial 'United Australia Party'.

It is understood by *The Advocate* that Mr Palmer signed off on the preselection this afternoon, making the discarded contraceptive the official UAP candidate for the seat of Maranoa at this year's federal election.

Hoisting the condom, still dripping with some responsible teenager's genetic material, high above his head today at the Lake Betoota Sailing Club, Clive told reporters that he's confident the latex cock sock has what it takes to defeat the incumbent Nationals member, David Littleproud.

'Just a few days ago, this condom was inside a box, sitting on some supermarket shelf in Betoota,' said Mr Palmer.

'Then, he and his other condom brothers were stuffed down the pants of some forward-thinking teen and walked right out of that supermarket. That's the type of go-getter attitude my party needs. To cap it all off, he was used for nearly a minute, then turned inside out and thrown against the roof of the bus. All without the driver batting an eyelid. Astounding.'

Clive then refused to answer any questions from the media as he proceeded to get a bit lost in the hallway of the sailing club.

A minder guided him to his car and they left.

More to come.

Hoisting the condom, still dripping with some responsible teenager's genetic material, high above his head today at the Lake Betoota Sailing Club, Clive told reporters that he's confident the latex cock sock has what it takes to defeat the incumbent Nationals member, David Littleproud.

Greens Volunteer Says He Knows It's, Like, Bad To Say This But Immigrants Only Vote Conservatively Because They Aren't That Well Educated

RICHIE MUND (27), a well-known vocal campaigner and son of two career high-paid public servants who have never had a financial worry in the world, says there's been a lot of government policy that can be blamed for the current trend of anti-intellectualism in Australian politics.

Number one, he says John Howard gutted education to keep the masses stupid, and two, the left have been overtaken by fruitless intersectionality focusing on women's rights and the experiences of immigrants and Aboriginal people.

'Like, don't get me wrong. I'm a big supporter of no flags, no borders, et cetera, et cetera … But right now, in this country … the rate of land clearing is catastrophic. It's got to get to the point where we are going to need to skim over the issues of these so-called minorities and focus on the immediate threats to our environment. Like, we can get back to all that stuff, but I'm sick of having to play identity politics while the reliability of wind power continues to be ignored.'

Richie, who volunteers for the Greens outside of his casually contracted job creating memes for GetUp, says that he could never tell his colleagues what he really thinks about the result of the 2017 gay marriage plebiscite and the subsequent re-election of the Liberal Party in New South Wales.

'I know it's like bad to say this but the reason immigrants and poor people and, like, bogan farmers, vote conservatively . . . it's because they aren't really that well educated unfortunately.'

Richie believes that when we can raise education standards in this country to the point where every man and woman have a similar quality of schooling as he and his mates did at Melbourne's Xavier College, then no one will ever vote Liberal again.

But for now, he's gotta wade through the murky waters of equality and affirmative action in order to save the world.

'Don't get me started on the ALLEGED examples of sexism I've been accused of in my office. Talk about a speed bump in my career.'

'Elon never got to where he was by having to worry about unfair power balances in the workplace,' says Richie.

Spunky Tasmanian Woman Is Wunhundroid Poircent Voting Fa Jacqui

A PROMINENT RURAL TASMANIAN grandmother of two with another on the way has today revealed to our reporters that she is making sure her vote counts, you can betcha bottom dollar on that.

Bronte Park (67) says after sevoin maybe oight Proime Ministoirs, she's 'had it arp to hoire', while gesturing to her flawlessly contoured cheekbones.

In fact, Bronte is so had it, she would vote for anyone else.

Luckily she doesn't have to do that.

Because, for arguably the first time in history, Bronte has a political voice that 100 per cent represents her fears, frustrations and hopes as a working-class lino-floor feminist from the great Apple Isle.

'And it ain't this boys' club I'm voting for,' she says, with a flicker of wild Huon pine burning in her iris.

With six boofhead sons looking for work, each with families to raise, Bronte knows a fucking six-storey art gallery isn't the only thing Tasmania has been calling out for.

'We noid woirk for woirking people. You ken all hold hands and sing "Kumbaya", boit the Libs will send the joibs to China, or even worse, the mainland.'

And as for Labor:

'Shorten hasn't visited us since fucken Beaconsfield.'

Bronte makes it very bloody clear where she stands on the Vote Compass.

'Jacqui has moi voite soigned, soiled, delivoired.'

Clive Palmer Vows To Build Full-Size Replica Of Notre Dame Cathedral On The Sunshine Coast

'We're in talks to rehire the Queensland Nickel staff here at Notre Dame Coolum. Others will be hired as sailors on my Titanic. I trust that answers your question! But due to budget constraints, Quasimodo will have to be replaced by a raptor from my dino park.'

LOCALLY UNPOPULAR POPULIST Clive Palmer, who is gunning for a seat in the lower house at this year's election, has responded to the ongoing disaster in Paris overnight that's seen one of the world's most iconic places of worship partially destroyed by fire.

The Notre Dame Cathedral in the French capital is hundreds of years old and is a favourite among the many millions of tourists that flock to Paris each year.

The republic's president, Emmanuel Macron, has called for an international effort to rebuild the cathedral.

It's a call that Clive Palmer has answered.

This morning on the Sunshine Coast, Palmer called a press conference out the front of his Coolum property where he outlined how he plans to help.

'Should I be elected to office, I promise to build a full-size replica of the Notre Dame church here in Coolum,' he said. 'The project will cost about half a billion dollars. Some will be mine and some will be the taxpayer's. It will be a bipartisan effort to rebuild this beautiful building. Or should I say, "biparisian"?'

A member of the local media cough-laughed.

'It will be built alongside my dinosaurs and it'll create jobs and attract tourism to the area. It's a small part of my plan for Queensland and Australia should the people choose to so graciously elect me to parliament again.'

A number of reporters asked him how this would affect his intent to pay the Queensland Nickel workers to whom he owes millions.

Clive also had an answer to that.

'We're in talks to rehire the Queensland Nickel staff here at Notre Dame Coolum. Others will be hired as sailors on my *Titanic*. I trust that answers your question! But due to budget constraints, Quasimodo will have to be replaced by a raptor from my dino park. I hope it spurs on a new version of the classic Disney movie: *The Velociraptor of Notre Dame*! Reeeeeeee! Reeeeeee! Hisssssssssss!'

Clive then shrugged and walked off without saying goodbye to anyone.

More to come.

Katter Candidate Resigns As Social Media Posts Emerge Of Him Working As A Barista In West End

THE KATTER AUSTRALIAN PARTY candidate for the seat of Yawannagokunt north-west of Brisbane has withdrawn after social media posts came to light that showed him once working in an inner city cafe.

Luke Hardt-Kennedy (35), a prominent rifle range supervisor and former Mackay Cutters superstar, has admitted to the allegations, stating that he needed to find some work while awaiting an ill-fated contract with the Broncos.

In a statement released by the KAP, Mr Hardt-Kennedy said the photos did not reflect his views today but that his actions were 'an important lesson for young people that your social media footprint will follow you'.

'It is clear the right thing for me to do is stand down,' the statement said.

'While I surrounded myself with those entitled, closed-minded people in West End many years ago and they in no way reflect the views I hold today, I understand, especially as a member of the Katter Party, that we need to be careful about what we share or like on social media.'

KAP leader, the Honourable Bob Katter III, says the images make him sick to the stomach.

'I'm glad Susie took the keys to my gun safe from me,' said the ropeable Member for Kennedy. 'The fact that this man has, at some point in his life, associated with residents of Boundary Street, is inexcusable.

'And I'm not talking about the Greeks or the blackfellas . . . or even the old Magpies players of West End. I'm talking full-blown white boys with dreadlocks. Luke Hardt-Kennedy is dead to me. He's been ordered to hand over his Akubra and Adler shotgun immediately.

'And I thought recruiting Fraser Anning was a bad call. Glad I dodged that bullet.'

More to come.

Report Finds Over 85 Per Cent Of Greens Voters Can Be Rehabilitated With A Hug From Dad

A RECENT STUDY by the AMA Queensland has found that the concerning rise of diagnosed Greens voters is one of the most easily avoidable epidemics since chlamydia hit the navy.

'It's easier to cure than the common cold,' says lead researcher Dr Derryn Thelps. 'But it requires cooperation and initiative from not only the sufferers, but also their families and the surrounding community.'

The report has found that thousands of detached, frustrated and bored sufferers of *ImightgivetheGreensago* could be cured immediately after a firm hug from Dad, and maybe a kiss

on the cheek, if they are of southern European background.

It is believed many young people could be harbouring the virus without showing direct symptoms.

'This ailment exists in a lot of young people. You know, especially with the urgent climate crisis our planet faces, and the fact that no one under the age of fifty can afford a home that isn't out the back of Bourke. However, these different factors don't necessarily manifest into a full-blown Greens voter, unless they have a fractured relationship with the strong male figures in their lives.'

Dr Thelps said that while some people didn't have father figures in their life, a hug from the high school principal on graduation day will more than suffice as a spot treatment.

Inner City Leftie Vows To Teach PM Lesson By Turning Safe Labor Seat Into Marginal Greens Seat

IN THE INNER CITY Betoota federal division of Mimimi, one local voter has today vowed to use his vote to teach Scott Morrison a lesson in the federal election next week.

How? By voting Greens in both the lower and upper house.

Wyatt Enrytchus (32) says he's never really thought much about the power he wields as a comfortable urban professional with a disposable income and 1.5 kids crammed into a heritage-defying rendered terrace house.

But after his favourite Prime Minister of all time was rolled in a messy Lib spill last August, he's been on a mission to oust the Nightwatchman that replaced him.

'We need to be focusing on tech and renewables,' says Wyatt. 'I come from a long line of Labor voters, but Turnbull had won me over from Shorten on that one, and now Morrison has effectively just run a 2007 Howard campaign. So, considering I am far too proud, and wealthy, to transition back to Labor …

'I'm voting Greens!'

While local Greens senator, Dr Rich Engay, was elected last time by stray votes from Wyatt's particular demographic – who usually feel too guilty to vote Green in both houses – 2019 looks like the year that inner Betoota's local Greens lower house candidate will finally leverage the support needed from this furious voter block of jaded enviro-bros and water birth mums.

However, what appears lost on voters like Wyatt is that all he's doing is undermining Labor's safe hold on his local area – and making it harder for them to overthrow a Morrison Government.

'Labor are a bit too, you know … uniony,' says Wyatt. 'A bit bogan. I know this seat has been Labor forever, but I don't work in a fucken factory. I'm voting Greens.'

Local Greens candidate Andy Vaxxer (22) says this is exactly the voter detachment he has been banking on.

'Just months ago I was a dereg-istered paramedic who was facing criminal charges for stealing and on-selling green whistles,' he says. 'Now I'm basically locked in for a six-figure salary for the next three years [haha].

'Remember, a vote for me is a vote for saying, fuck you, ScoMo!'

One Nation Adds New Dot Point To Their Vetting Process For Potential Candidates

AS OF TODAY, One Nation will be adding a third dot point to their thorough background checks for potential political candidates, which previously had only required answers to whether or not they had ever killed anyone or harboured the sufficient hatred for Muslims and Africans.

One Nation Senate candidate for Queensland Steve Dickson has resigned after footage was released of him making derogatory comments and touching a dancer in a US strip club.

Mr Dickson said in a statement he apologised sincerely for his behaviour, before resigning, stating that he's realised you can't come back from something this fucking embarrassing.

The vision was recorded during an undercover investigation by Al Jazeera but aired for the first time by Nine's *A Current Affair* on Monday.

It was filmed as part of the same operation which last month revealed Mr Dickson and party advisor James Ashby travelled to the US last year

seeking millions of dollars in foreign donations from lobby groups like the National Rifle Association (NRA).

The newly released recordings showed Mr Dickson talking disparagingly about the dancers with fellow patrons. He refers to one dancer as a 'bitch' and says of another: 'Little tits, nothing there.'

Mr Dickson is also filmed as saying: 'I think white women fuck a whole lot better, they know what they're doing. Asian chicks don't. I've done more

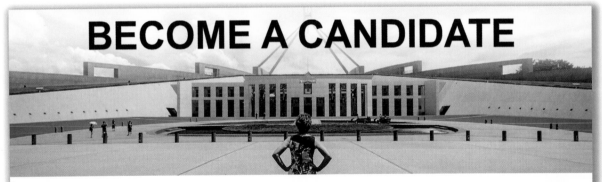

REQUIREMENTS

• I have never killed anyone

• I'm not that into immigrants

• I'm unlikely to get fucken blind in a US strip club while groping and the soliciting their employees to suck me off for cash, before openly admitting to a stranger that I frequently root Asian sex workers despite being married ***

Asian than I know what to do with.'

Another segment shows him talking with a dancer after slipping money into her lingerie.

'You need to slide your hand on my cock,' he says to the dancer.

'Right now?' she asks.

'Yeah absolutely,' he responds.

She declines, saying: 'I can't do that, sorry, they'll probably notice.'

In his statement today, Dickson said he was deeply remorseful for his 'disrespectful comments towards women'.

One Nation leader Pauline Hanson said she has accepted Mr Dickson's resignation, and has made moves to immediately update the far-right party's thorough vetting process.

'I'm upset with this, Steve is a family man ... I'm sorry he is deeply upset by this, I'm not going to judge him any further.'

The new background check for candidates now includes a question asking potential candidates if they are 'unlikely to get fucken blind in a

US strip club while groping and then soliciting their employees to suck me off for cash, before openly admitting to a stranger that I frequently root Asian sex workers despite being married'.

'It's necessary,' said Hanson, who lost all four of her senate candidates to citizenship scandals and dissent within 18 months of the last election.

'I'm also in half a mind to check their likelihood of allowing an undercover journalist to follow them for an entire year with a hidden camera.'

Explorers Shocked To Discover Palmer United Leaflets At The Bottom Of The Mariana Trench

IN A SAD INDICTMENT on the state of the planet we call home, some US explorers have today discovered rubbish at the deepest point under the sea.

On the deepest dive ever made by a human inside a submarine, Victor Vescovo, a retired naval officer and Texas-based investor, made the saddening discovery of rubbish at the bottom of the Mariana Trench today.

The diver explained how shocked and saddened he was to discover the Palmer United Party leaflets at the deepest point in the ocean.

'I was crushed,' explained Vescovo from his sat phone in the middle of the Pacific Ocean. 'At a moment when I should have been celebrating an incredible feat, I was reminded of the devastating effect mankind is having on this planet.'

Vescovo then explained that he was somewhat confused as to how the laminated leaflet made its way down there without disintegrating, and who the obnoxious smiling man on the paper was.

'But one of my crew is from your country of Queensland,' said Vescovo,

muddling things up slightly as many Americans tend to do. 'And he explained to me who this guy who doesn't pay his workers is, and how much of a bin fire his entry to politics was a few years ago and how he is trying it on again.

'Hopefully people don't go for the baseless promises of things like 300-kilometre-per-hour bullet trains across the country and we don't have any more of his pamphlets floating down into the ocean in future.'

Lambie Promises Royal Commission Into Whether Regional Tasmanian AFL Umpires Are Fucken Blind

INDEPENDENT SENATE CAN-DIDATE Jacqui Lambie has come out strong with some big promises just days before Tasmania joins the rest of the country at the polls.

Eighteen months after having to resign from the federal Senate due to her never-before-considered dual-citizenship status, Lambie is back and more Australian than ever.

Tasmania has six sitting senators up for election – three from Labor, one Liberal, a National and a Green – with Jacqui backing herself to peel the job off the latter two.

Speaking today at a press conference from the sideline of one of her nephews' representative Aussie rules matches, Lambie has revealed that she's not messing around – and has vowed to tackle the issues that are close to the hearts of all regional *Tasmoiiinians*.

Namely, the standard of volunteer umpires on the sidelines at provincial matches.

'How are our boys supposed to make the big time in Melbourne and Perth if the umpires are constantly getting the calls wrong?' she said. 'If elected into the Senate, I promise to call for a royal commission into whether the umpires out this way are fucken blind.'

The proposed inquiry will also cover the possibility that if, in fact, some of the umpires are fucken blind, are they only getting away with it because their eyes are fucken painted on?

Other campaign policies also look to combat 'revenue-razing' highway cops and the increased threats of violence on the Burnie Buy Swap N Sell Facebook page.

> *The proposed inquiry will also cover the possibility that if, in fact, some of the umpires are fucken blind, are they only getting away with it because their eyes are fucken painted on?*

Malcolm And Lucy Turnbull Laugh Hysterically To Themselves Before Voting For Clive Palmer

NORTH BONDI PRIMARY SCHOOL stood still this afternoon as former Prime Minister Malcolm Turnbull and his former Lord Mayor of Sydney Lucy Turnbull climbed out of an unmarked Range Rover to take part in the democratic process.

Turnbull, the most recently ousted Prime Minister to have previously defeated Bill Shorten at the polls did not appear to be wearing any Liberal Party paraphernalia such as t-shirts, pins or headwear.

After giving his Liberal Party successor Dave Sharma a wide berth at the front gate, the eastern suburbs power couple headed straight to the ballot.

AEC staff described their affluent giggles as 'chilling' before both Malcolm and Lucy filled in their ballot papers with what appeared to be a clear protest vote.

'Well, I spent the last five years publicly berating Bill Shorten, so I'm not voting for Labor,' laughed Turnbull. 'That would be a pointless vote in this electorate anyway. Look at these people.' Turnbull then gestured to his fellow Wentworth constituents. 'Do any of them look like they give a fuck about workers' rights or free health care [hahaha]?'

Lucy Turnbull agreed.

'I mean, the ship Malcolm jumped out of was burning to the hull and full of explosives,' she said. 'But Shorten [hahahaha]?'

Mr Turnbull then went on to insinuate that the couple were effectively voting against both major parties.

'I think it's time to make Australia great . . .' said Malcolm Turnbull. 'Hint hint!'

Lucy Turnbull joined in on the jokes.

'Or fat [hahahaha].'

At time of press, both Turnbulls were seen in the back seat of their private car, driving back up the Bondi bottleneck for a late lunch with the Paspaley family at the Woolloomooloo wharves.

'Look at these people . . . Do any of them look like they give a fuck about workers' rights or free health care [hahaha]?'

Clive Palmer's Failed Election Campaign Leaves Nation Facing Critical Yellow Ink Shortage

EVEN AFTER SPENDING close to $60 million on advertising, Clive Palmer's United Australia Party is set to miss out on a Senate seat, even in Queensland where he has plastered even more billboards in comparison to the rest of the country.

In the lower house, his candidates won 3.4 per cent of the vote nationally. In Queensland, his party was easily outvoted by One Nation, which received 8.4 per cent of the vote compared to Mr Palmer's 3.5 per cent. It's a notable dip since the 2013 election, where they polled 5.49 per cent nationally and 9.89 per cent in Queensland.

This election, he has won 389,888 votes across Australia, at basically $150 per vote.

What Clive gets out of this expensive affair is yet to be seen.

Some say he has gifted the Coalition their landslide win by splitting the vote and smearing Bill Shorten's name across the country, in an effort to secure coalmining-related special treatment down the track.

Others say he's effectively just pulled $60 million out of an ATM and thrown it at passing traffic.

However, one very real result is the fact that Australia is now facing a nationwide shortage of yellow ink.

Prominent signage franchises, Officeworks, Bannerama, Snap Printing and outdoor advertisers APN have all reported a critically low supply of yellow ink.

'It's making it very hard for us to service our other fatboy clients like Maccas and Hungrys,' said one corflute manufacturer. 'We've got much more long-term clients who actually advertise successfully complaining about why their logos are orange! And he didn't even win us a seat. All he's done is send our entire industry broke. Like he will do to the tourism operators on the reef when ScoMo gives him that mine he just paid for.'

Picture Credits

Page 2: Shutterstock; p 4 Nik Walker p 7-8, Shutterstock; p 9, Shutterstock; p 13 Shutterstock; p 14 Shutterstock; p 15 Shutterstock; p 16 Shutterstock; p 17 Facebook / Joshua Gane; p 18 Shutterstock; p 19 Shutterstock; p 20 Shutterstock; p 21 Shutterstock; p 22 Shutterstock; p 23 Diamantina Consolidated Holdings Pty Ltd; p 25 Shutterstock; p 26 Shutterstock; p 27 AAP / Roy Hill, Shutterstock; p 28 Diamantina Consolidated Holdings Pty Ltd; p 31 Shutterstock; p 32 Shutterstock; p 33 Shutterstock; p 34 Diamantina Consolidated Holdings Pty Ltd; p 35 Diamantina Consolidated Holdings Pty Ltd; p 36 Diamantina Consolidated Holdings Pty Ltd; p 37 Diamantina Consolidated Holdings Pty Ltd; p 38 Diamantina Consolidated Holdings Pty Ltd; p 39 Diamantina Consolidated Holdings Pty Ltd; p 41 Diamantina Consolidated Holdings Pty Ltd; p 42 AAP / Lukas Coch; p 43 Diamantina Consolidated Holdings Pty Ltd; p 44 Diamantina Consolidated Holdings Pty Ltd; p 45 Diamantina Consolidated Holdings Pty Ltd; p 46 Shutterstock; p 47 Shutterstock; p 48 AAP / Brendan Esposito; p 51 Diamantina Consolidated Holdings Pty Ltd; p 52 Diamantina Consolidated Holdings Pty Ltd; p 53 AAP / Mick Tsikas, Shutterstock; p 54 Diamantina Consolidated Holdings Pty Ltd; p 55 AAP / Tracey Nearmy; p 56 AAP / Lukas Coch; p 57 Shutterstock; p 58 Diamantina Consolidated Holdings Pty Ltd; p 59 Diamantina Consolidated Holdings Pty Ltd; p 60 AAP / Brendan Esposito; p 61 Diamantina Consolidated Holdings Pty Ltd; p 62 Shutterstock; p 63 Diamantina Consolidated Holdings Pty Ltd; p 64 Diamantina Consolidated Holdings Pty Ltd; p 65 Shutterstock; p 66 Shutterstock; p 69 Shutterstock; p 70 Shutterstock; p 71 Diamantina Consolidated Holdings Pty Ltd; p 72 Diamantina Consolidated Holdings Pty Ltd; p 73 Diamantina Consolidated Holdings Pty Ltd; p 74 Shutterstock; p 75 Shutterstock; p 76 AAP / Tracey Nearmy; --p 79 Shutterstock; p 80 Diamantina Consolidated Holdings Pty Ltd; p 81 Diamantina Consolidated Holdings Pty Ltd; p 82 Diamantina Consolidated Holdings Pty Ltd; p 83 Diamantina Consolidated Holdings Pty Ltd; p 84 AAP / Tracey Nearmy; p 85 Diamantina Consolidated Holdings Pty Ltd; p 86 Diamantina Consolidated Holdings Pty Ltd; p 87 Shutterstock; p 88 AAP / Marlon Dalton; p 90 Diamantina Consolidated Holdings Pty Ltd; p 91 Diamantina Consolidated Holdings Pty Ltd; p 92 Diamantina Consolidated Holdings Pty Ltd; p 93 AAP / Dan Peled; p 94 Shutterstock; p 97 Shutterstock; p 98 AAP / Joel Carrett; p 99 Diamantina Consolidated Holdings Pty Ltd; p 100 Diamantina Consolidated Holdings Pty Ltd; p 102 Shutterstock; p 103 Diamantina Consolidated Holdings Pty Ltd; p 104 Diamantina Consolidated Holdings Pty Ltd; p 105 Diamantina Consolidated Holdings Pty Ltd; p 106 Diamantina Consolidated Holdings Pty Ltd; p 107 Shutterstock; p 108 AAP / Paul Tyquin; p 111 Shutterstock; p 113 AAP / David Crosling, Shutterstock; p 114 Shutterstock; p 115 AAP / James Ross; p 116 Diamantina Consolidated Holdings Pty Ltd; p 117 AAP / David Moir; p 118 Diamantina Consolidated Holdings Pty Ltd; p 119 Diamantina Consolidated Holdings Pty Ltd; p 120 Shutterstock; p 121 Diamantina Consolidated Holdings Pty Ltd; p 122 AAP / Glenn Hunt; p 125 AAP / Dan Peled; p 126 AAP / Alex Ellinghausen; p 127 Shutterstock; p 128 Shutterstock; p 129 AAP / Lukas Coch; p 130 Shutterstock; p 131 Shutterstock; p 132 Diamantina Consolidated Holdings Pty Ltd; p 133 AAP / Mick Tsikas; p 134 AAP / Lukas Coch; p 135 AAP / Lukas Coch; p 136 Diamantina Consolidated Holdings Pty Ltd; p 137 AAP / Mick Tsikas; p 138 AAP / Darren England; p 139 Diamantina Consolidated Holdings Pty Ltd; p 140 AAP / Craig Golding, Diamantina Consolidated Holdings Pty Ltd; p 143 Diamantina Consolidated Holdings Pty Ltd; p 144 Diamantina Consolidated Holdings Pty Ltd; p 145 Diamantina Consolidated Holdings Pty Ltd, Shutterstock; p 146 Shutterstock; p 148 Diamantina Consolidated Holdings Pty Ltd; p 149 AAP / Lukas Coch; p 150 AAP / Sam Mooy; p 151 Diamantina Consolidated Holdings Pty Ltd; p 152 Shutterstock; p 153 Diamantina Consolidated Holdings Pty Ltd, Shutterstock; p 154 Shutterstock; p 155 Diamantina Consolidated Holdings Pty Ltd; p 156 LadBible; p 157 Shutterstock; p 158 Shutterstock; p 161 Shutterstock; p 162 Shutterstock; p 163 Shutterstock; p 164 Shutterstock; p 165 Shutterstock; p 166 Shutterstock; p 167 Shutterstock; p 168 Shutterstock; p 170 Shutterstock; p 171 Shutterstock; p 172 Diamantina Consolidated Holdings Pty Ltd ;p 173 Shutterstock; p 174 Shutterstock; p 175 Shutterstock; p 176 Shutterstock; p 177 Shutterstock; p 178 Shutterstock; p 179 Shutterstock; p 180 Shutterstock; p 181 Shutterstock; p 182 Shutterstock; p 183 Shutterstock; p 184 Shutterstock; p 185 Shutterstock; p 186 Diamantina Consolidated Holdings Pty Ltd; p 189 Samuel Condon; p 190 Diamantina Consolidated Holdings Pty Ltd; p 191 AAP / Dave Hunt; p 192 Shutterstock; p 194 Diamantina Consolidated Holdings Pty Ltd; p 195 Diamantina Consolidated Holdings Pty Ltd; p 197 Shutterstock; p 198 AAP / Glenn Hunt; p 200 Diamantina Consolidated Holdings Pty Ltd; p 201 Diamantina Consolidated Holdings Pty Ltd; p 202 Diamantina Consolidated Holdings Pty Ltd; p 203 Shutterstock; p 204 Diamantina Consolidated Holdings Pty Ltd, Shutterstock; p 206 Shutterstock; p 207 Shutterstock; p 209 Diamantina Consolidated Holdings Pty Ltd; p 210 Diamantina Consolidated Holdings Pty Ltd; p 211 Facebook / Jacqui Lambie; p 212 Diamantina Consolidated Holdings Pty Ltd; p 213 Shutterstock

First published 2019 in Macmillan
by Pan Macmillan Australia Pty Limited
Level 25, 1 Market Street, Sydney, New South Wales
Australia 2000

A CIP catalogue record for this book is available from the National Library of Australia:
http://catalogue.nla.gov.au

Design by Arielle Gamble
Colour + reproduction by Splitting Image Colour Studio
Printed in Singapore

We advise that the information contained in this book does not negate personal responsibility on the part of the reader for their own health and safety. It is recommended that individually tailored advice is sought from your healthcare or medical professional. The publishers and their respective employees, agents and authors are not liable for injuries or damage occasioned to any person as a result of reading or following the information contained in this book.

10 9 8 7 6 5 4 3 2 1